October 6, 2014

To Norma,

Thank you for helping
me clean up my act.

Always love and
forever laughter,

Lola

1-800-557-LOLA
(5652)
Fax: (949) 499-9870   Phone: (949) 499-1968
Email: lola@laughandlearn.org
Website: www.laughandlearn.org

Laughter
Made From
Experience

Laughter
Made From
Experience

*"Every statement of fact that
you read in this book is
based on true experience.
You can trust me.
I'm a woman."*

by
Lola Gillebaard

STRATFORD BOOKS
Winston-Salem, North Carolina
2008

INTRODUCTION

These vignettes are collected from the writing and and the presentations which Lola has done during her career as a humorist. That career includes keynote speeches at national conventions, one-woman shows, motivational talks for business people and entertaining ones for cruise-ship vacationers, programs for breast cancer survivors and medical professionals, and even a brief sally into standup comedy.

Taken together, they tell the story of the author's life from the little girl with a leg brace entering first grade, through marriage and migration across the country, to raising four sons and losing beloved parents. Experiences common to most women gain fresh meaning from Lola's close scrutiny splashed with humor.

Though its outlook is comedic, this collection touches sadness as well, because that, too, is a part of life. Lola says that people often have the misconception that humorists laugh all the time. "Not true," she says, "To know how to be truly glad, one must know how to be truly sad." Perhaps the key word is *truly*. Lola learned long ago that "only the truth is funny"

To Mom and Dad, my husband Hank, and our four sons—who created the settings for these stories.

THE LAST BITE

I cried at your funeral last Monday, but I smiled this morning when I read the letter you wrote to me the night before you died. You had the last word, Mom, as always. On the day that I was born, the doctor said I'd never walk. You said I would.

Several years later, I screamed when you ordered me to put one foot in front of the other—then threatened me with a switch if I didn't.

"It's hard," I yelled.

"So's life," you said. "Now walk."

I did. Then I fell down. You helped me up, and I saw tears in your eyes. Again, you waved the switch in the air, and I walked.

Later in life, I hated the brace. When you strapped it on, I tried to think of how good you smelled instead of how sweaty the leather brace smelled. I loved to watch you move. You almost danced. Your hair bounced and your legs looked pretty in your high-heeled shoes.

"Pretty is as pretty does," you said. You said it on a day when you curled my hair and I wore the dotted swiss dress and you caught me admiring myself in the mirror. My little mirror was my favorite. It wasn't long enough to show my legs.

That was the same day I sat on the minister's lap when he came to call. While he was purring about what a sweet little girl I was, I put his index finger between my teeth and bit down till he bled. I turned to you and said, "You told me to bite back." The minister kept his distance after that.

The day before I started school, I said to you, "If anybody asks about my leg, I'm gonna tell 'em it's none of their business." "You do and I'll wear you out," you threatened. You meant it, too; you never joked about spankings. When you picked me up at school after that first day, you asked, "Well, did anyone mention your leg?" "No, Mom," I said. And no one did. After the first week, I forgot about my leg.

During those early years, my favorite dream was the one in which I tap-danced in high heels, a bathing suit, and a top hat. You didn't know about my dream, but you saw to it that I took dancing lessons on Mondays and Thursdays. In fact, the dancing teacher lived with us for a while. I dreaded those nights at the supper table when you asked Miss Van Tassle, "How was dancing class today?" She always said, "Fine," but she never looked at me when she said it.

We had a "Mistress Mary" dance recital coming up, and both Miss Van Tassle and I knew that I was the most uncoordinated cockle shell that ever grew in Mistress Mary's garden. Sure enough, on the night of the performance, my ballet slipper came off and I fell down while Mistress Mary was watering her flowers. Afterwards, I told you that I would never be in another dance recital, and you knew I meant it.

In the fourth grade, I tried out for the yearly minstrel show. When Miss Bobbitt called out the people in the cast, my name wasn't on the list, and I told you about it that night at the supper table. You excused yourself and went upstairs. The next day, Miss Bobbitt read the list again. My name was on it. I performed much better sitting down as an end man in blackface than as a cockle shell standing up in ballet shoes.

That was the year I had my second operation and the brace came off. I was ten years old. For the first time in my life, I got to wear saddle shoes. For the first time in my life, I was 'like everybody else.'

At least I was until I went to camp that summer. My best friend and I were walking down the hill to our cabin, when someone hollered from the window of a nearby cabin, "What's the matter with your leg?" And then her cabin mate said, "Yeah, why're you limping?"

I didn't know what they were talking about. I didn't know what 'limping' meant. And then I remembered what I had seen on the camp's medical form. On the line called "Handicaps," you had written "slight limp." You had never mentioned a limp to me, and I had wondered what it meant when I saw it. But I hadn't asked you—just the way I wouldn't ask you about sex later on.

That two weeks at camp proved to be the most miserable fourteen days of my life. Once I realized that I walked funny, I walked even funnier. My whole body and spirit became involved in trying to put one foot in front of the other without dragging the left one. I was furious with you and determined to make you sorry you'd ever written "slight limp" on that form. I'd show you, Mom, by winning the Best Camper award, then you'd be sorry. I joined in every activity the camp offered. I ran. I danced. I swam. I fell down. I got up. I smiled. I hated you. I wanted to bite your index finger completely off. And I won the award.

When I got home, I showed it to you, but I never told you the rest of the story. You were pleased but not at all surprised. "That's nice," you said, sorting my grimy clothes for the wash. But it was you, quietly and taking great pains to place it just right, who sewed the Best Camper patch onto my windbreaker.

I remembered my two weeks at camp many years later, after you fell, injuring your head and breaking your hip and ankle. At age eighty-five, you were still looking forward to life, even though you missed Dad after his death. And then you fell.

The next time I saw you, your leg was in a cast and a pin was in your hip. Your hair didn't bounce because your head had been shaved, but little ringlets were already emerging from your scalp. You were in your own bed at home and when the nurse urged you to get up and walk, you turned your face to the wall. You got up only to go bathroom.

"Mom, the doctor says that you must exercise."

"You don't know how sick I've been. Two blood clots removed."

"But, Mom, the doctor says you can't get better unless you force yourself to walk."

"It's too hard."

"So's life, Mom. Remember?" You thought a moment and nodded your head.

"Mom, I promised the therapist I'd have you on your feet when he got here." I could feel my voice rising as I continued, "Do I have to go out and get a switch?"

Smiling, you raised yourself in bed and slowly swung your legs toward the floor. I kissed you. Moments later, with great effort, you were taking a few small steps. And smiling even more.

I smiled, too, as I read the letter you had written to me several years and many steps later: "Thanks, Sweetheart, thanks for biting me back."

HE·E·E·RE'S SONNY!

I can't believe it. I've always wanted to be on the Tonight Show with Johnny Carson. And here I am standing in the wings with my Number Three son. Not that
I'm part of the show exactly, but I'm holding a cup of
coffee just like the rest of the backstage crew.

My son squeezes my hand. "Here he comes," he
whispers. I turn around, and there stands The Man. Swal-
lowing the lump in my throat, I say, "Hi, Johnny."

"Hi," Johnny answers. Then he looks me straight in
the eye and says three little words I shall never forget:
"Who are you?"

Before I can answer, Ed McMahon bellows, "He-e-
e-ere's Johnny!" and Carson rushes onstage. Now that's
show biz!

I give my son's hand a squeeze of approval. This
kid hardly ever wears socks or underwear, but he knows
how to live by the seat of his pants. Today at NBC he has
on his good pants—the pants that graduated from high
school with him last June—and he looks and smells like a
model in an after-shave commercial.

Members of the backstage crew nod, recognizing
him because he's been here several times before. And
for that, he gives credit to the Policeman's Ball Association. But I'm getting ahead of myself. Time for what we
in the writing business call a flashback.

A year ago, my son and a friend drove to Burbank
to see their idol, Johnny Carson. When they reached the

NBC studies, people waiting in line for tickets to Johnny's show stretched halfway around the building. The boys spotted two girls in the line with four tickets, who welcomed them as if they were expected. Unfortunately the audience was filled just after the girls walked inside, leaving two boys at the head of a new line–going nowhere.

They sauntered around the building where a rear entrance was manned by a single guard. The boys crouched behind some shrubbery and watched. People who entered the building spoke to the guard and flashed something inside their wallets. The boys couldn't hear what was said or see what the wallets held.

The schemers left the bushes and went to the parking lot to think. They sat by a lamp post and went through their wallets. Driver's licenses, library cards, and Social Security cards were were too obvious, and they knew that NBC's colors were red and blue. Suddenly his friend began to search around the lot as if he had a purpose.

And he did–an unwrinkled and unsmudged sticker reading "NBC STUDIO TOURS" across the top. Just then, my son found something behind the homecoming queen's photo: his ID card from the Police Association when he had delivered tickets to their benefit ball. It was bordered in red and blue.

Now it was his turn to explore the parking lot. He found a flat piece of glass in a trash can and used it to cut "NBC STUDIOS" neatly off the sticker, and pressed them to his Police Association card. Taking a minute to admire their handiwork, they decided to give it a try.

My son loped toward the guard, held his breath, flashed his open wallet, and smiled. "Hi, how's it going?"

The guard looked first at him and then at his friend. "Is he with you?"

"Yeah," said my son.

And that was it.

The two boys started down the long hallway as if they knew where they were going. My son whispered, "Hang a right." They did.

They found themselves in the midst of a party. The table was decorated with an ice sculpture surrounded by champagne, iced shrimp, and Swedish meatballs. People were laughing and chattering.

For a moment, the boys looked as if they had just discovered girls, but before anyone noticed, they regained their casual cool.

His friend speared a meatball, and he opened a Coke. They nodded at people chatting on the other side of the table. Then a woman approached my son.

"Pardon me," she said.

"Hi, how's it going?" he said quickly.

"Oh, fine," the woman said, "but I have to ask you something."

He smiled, holding his breath again.

"Isn't Robert Smith your father?" the woman asked. "You look just like him."

My son smiled his largest one and said, "Thank you."

Just then, someone waved to the woman and she left. He exhaled. Later, he discovered that Robert Smith was a writer for "The Tonight Show."

The boys left the party and started back down the hall—this time hanging a left. Another long corridor with large rooms on both sides stretched before them. The doors were open, so they went into each one. They saw sets being constructed and looked in on the taping studios for "The Midnight Special," "The John Davidson Show," and "Hollywood Squares." (Later, these ever-so-casual visitors could be seen jumping up and down in the parking lot, shrieking about all they'd seen.)

Continuing along, they spotted a man and a woman coming out of a doorway with a red light over it. Catching the door before it clicked shut, the boys walked in.

The room was much darker than the hallway, but they could see people roaming around holding cups of coffee. A big picture of Johnny Carson was on the wall. Two TV sets were tuned to "The Tonight Show." They were facing an opening that led onto the stage! Carson was doing his monologue. They looked behind and saw the same monologue on the TV screens. That's when they knew for sure that they were seeing a real "Tonight" taping. As my son said later, "Mom, it's really awesome. Come with me sometime." I was appalled at his audacity, and told him so.

Since then, he'd taken several of his classmates to the Burbank studios. Just before graduation, he escorted the homecoming queen to Studio 1. He was becoming a high school celebrity, and I was becoming curious.

So now, I'm his accomplice, standing in the wings, sipping coffee, and watching the show. I'm not sure which thrills me more—seeing Johnny Carson in person, or knowing that my son is wearing socks and underwear. Actually, it's neither. The big moment was when my son flashed his wallet at the entrance and told the guard, "She's with me."

What Matters the Price of Gold?

I hate to polish silver. I also hate to see it tarnished. When the second hate overpowers the first, I groan and pull out the jar of silver foam, turn on the radio, then I rub. That's what I was doing recently when the newscaster announced the current price of gold, followed by the current price of silver.

My rubbing motion slowed. I gazed more fondly at the silver. No matter how much the price may fluctuate, I was cleaning up a fortune. I rinsed the heavy coffee server with hot water and dried it carefully. Then I picked up my favorite piece: a silver utensil for brewing hot tea. On the end of the long handle is an ornate windmill whose blades turn when flicked. Mama and Papa gave it to us soon after we were married. I watched the tiny windmill spin round and round and thought of those two.

They were married in Amsterdam in 1920. Her wedding present to him was a legacy that had belonged to Mama's grandfather, a gold watch sprinkled with diamonds and rubies. When a button was pressed, the watch would chime the time. The chime was as hearty as a tulip and always accurate. The heirloom was made in 1790, a technological wonder for its time. Papa gave Mama a gold diamond bracelet. The diamonds clustered all the way around it, even covering the safety catch.

Mama and Papa had their ups and downs, but they loved each other and parented five children. In 1940, when the oldest child was fourteen years old, Holland was occupied by the Germans for five years of World War II. Soon after, food rationing began. The Gillebaard family, like most families in Amsterdam, learned to live with scarcity. People started to buy anything of value, particularly gold, diamonds, and silver.

In September of '44, the Allied air invasion of Arnhem cut off the Dutch industrial west, the most densely populated portion of Holland. As a result, food rations for the Gillebaard family of seven were two pounds of sugar beets, two pounds of potatoes, and one loaf of bread per person each week. Dutch guilders bought the rationed food and paid the rent. For any other purchase, inflation made money almost worthless.

My husband Hank was seventeen years old then. He weighed eighty-five pounds. Mama's sugar beet and potato soup was mostly water by the middle of the week. One night after sending the children to bed hungry, Mama slipped something into Papa's pocket. Papa protested, but Mama insisted.

The next morning, Papa swapped Mama's diamond bracelet on the black market for a goat—supposedly a milk goat. The goat was delivered in the middle of the night and put into the attic of their home.

Now Papa was a businessman, not a farmer. But that night he went to the attic with a footstool and a pail. He looked like a man who knew exactly what he was about. The truth was, Papa had never milked a cow, let alone a goat.

The goat was white, with electric blue eyes. Papa's eyes were electric blue, too. Man and animal glared at each other. Papa sat on the stool and pulled at what he thought were the proper appendages for milk. The goat bleated and took off for the farthest corner of the attic.

Papa picked up the pail and stool, walked over and placed the pail underneath the goat, the stool beside. The goat glared. Papa sat and pulled. The goat bleated and kicked Papa in the stomach. Then the animal knocked over the pail and raced to the opposite corner of the room.

The family was waiting at the bottom of the steps as Papa came down. Beads of perspiration rolled off his neck. He turned up the empty pail and said, "There's not a drop of milk in there. That crazy goat is dry."

And then Papa started back up the steps. He was carrying an axe. He slammed the attic door behind him. They all heard him say, "I'm sorry, I have to do this."

Mama and the children listened to the hooves of the goat touch down as he loped back and forth across the floor, bleating frantically. Between bleats, Papa's determined footsteps could be heard and the sound of his voice as he talked to the goat. Then more bleats, more hooves, louder talking.

Finally, the goat's bleating drowned out the other sounds. The attic door opened. Papa backed through the door still talking to the goat. He held the axe behind his back. His shirt was torn and his hand was bleeding.

"That damn goat is alive and well," he said. Mama bandaged his hand in a piece of sheeting.

Papa went next door. The man had owned a butcher shop before meat had withdrawn to the black market.

The neighbor killed and skinned the goat. His price was half the carcass, but he did not split the carcass lengthwise. He took the bottom half.

And so Mama's priceless gold diamond bracelet bought the Gillebaard family the top half of a milkless goat. Mama prepared goat stew, goat hash, and goat soup. Every meal was a feast.

By February of 1945, the goat was remembered fondly. Food rations had dwindled to half a loaf of bread and two potatoes per person per week. Mama supplemented the family diet with boiled tulip bulbs when she was lucky enough to find them. The weather was freezing, and there was no wood or coal to burn. The Gillebaards, like most Dutch, were slowly starving.

One Sunday afternoon, Papa and one of his employees bicycled to the farmland outside of Amsterdam. They pedaled on tire rims—all rubber had been confiscated many months before.

Knocking on the door of every farm house, they asked each farmer if he had food to sell. Papa would pull out his antique gold watch, which now was all he had to trade for nourishment. The farmer would examine the watch, listen to the chimes, then shake his head, "I've got gold coming out of my ears." With that said, he would slam the door.

Papa and his employee turned up their coat collars against the wind and continued to cycle. Then they found a farmer who looked not at the watch, but at the two men. "What can you do?" he asked.

Papa's employee said that he was a carpenter. The farmer smiled and said, "There's work for you."The farmhouse was also without heat, and he wanted every crack in the house filled to insulate against the cold. Papa helped as best he could. The farmer gave the two men four sacks of beans. By the time they loaded the beans on the bicycles, the light of the wintry day was disappearing.

"Let me see that watch again," the farmer said. Papa's heart pounded. He held out the watch in the palm of his hand. He pressed the chime. The farmer listened, his hands propped on his hips. "I've got enough diamonds and gold to open a jewelry store of my own, but I'll give you a sack of beans for the watch."

Papa said, "Make it two."

"One sack of beans. That's it."

Papa thought about the seven stomachs he yearned to fill. He said, "I'll take the beans."

The Gillebaard family survived, and Papa told that story many times. He always ended by saying, "The skills of labor are worth more than precious gold."

And so today, what matters the price of gold and silver? In time of need, what will they buy? A sack of beans? A milkless goat? I turned off the radio and put the gleaming silver where it belonged.

A GOOSE IS COOKED

The energy crisis peaked right in my kitchen, one automatic gadget at a time. The counter tops were beginning to look like the housewares department of a discount store just before a going-out-of-business sale. In fact, the only movable object that didn't require plugging in was my husband Hank, who was self-propelled—especially when shopping for more gadgets!

When we first set up housekeeping, our only electrical appliance was an automatic pop-up toaster. Hank loved it. At breakfast he'd gaze dreamily into the coiled slots and, when the bell dinged, he'd jump up right along with the toast.

Our next investment was an automatic coffee maker. When Hank wasn't mesmerized by the toaster at breakfast, he'd get a kick out of watching the water turn golden brown as it dripped down. Then came the juicer. Its piercing whir was a melodic counterpoint to the syncopated drip of the coffee maker and the staccato pop of the toaster.

But the star soloist of our breakfast orchestra became, soon after its purchase, our automatic egg cooker: "Boils eggs as simple as one-two-three." The "one, two, three" part was right, but the process was anything but simple. It went like this: one, find a straight pin to puncture a hole in the large end of the egg so it can breathe while boiling; two, place the punctured end downward so it can boil while breathing; three, put a teaspoon of water around each three-minute egg (shorter or longer cooking time requiring different amounts of water). Dutifully, I stored the appropriate measuring spoons inside the cooker, along with a supply of straight pins. On one occasion, however, Hank forgot to remove the paraphernalia before he plugged in the cooker. No eggs were served that morning, but we had enough sterile instruments to perform surgery.

We reserved the bacon cooker and the waffle iron for use on Saturdays, Sundays, and legal holidays, when our breakfast table resembled a window display at an appliance store. Between the sizzling bacon and the sticking waffle iron, Hank didn't need the morning paper to keep him occupied; a baton to conduct our orchestra would have done nicely.

The day he brought home the blender was another occasion. That blender grated, chopped, stirred, ground, pureed, whipped, mixed, blended, liquified, and frappéd— or so Hank reported, breathlessly. He was so excited about having ten choices for preparing food that he took a head of cauliflower and tried each speed, watching the blades go round and round. At last, the final product emerged: cauliflower juice.

Our next three automatic wonders were a hamburger cooker, a hot-dog cooker, and a peanut-butter maker. Therein lie three more tales. A hamburger cooker is great if you are alone in the house and don't feel like walking to the local fast-food stand. For feeding a family of six—forget it. By the time you get around to serving the third, the first is ready for seconds, and the sixth has fled to Burger King for firsts.

Nor has the hot-dog maker exactly worked out. It holds six dogs, but cooks them so fast that they shrivel up. Thus, it takes two hot dogs to make one serving. That leaves the peanut-butter maker. Now, all supermarkets offer smooth peanut butter, chunky peanut butter, and so-called "old-fashioned" peanut butter. Right? But our peanut-butter maker produces only its own middling variety, a jar of glob too thick for a milk shake but much too runny for a peanut butter and jelly sandwich. We stored the machine in the cupboard—for future reference.

One day, the inevitable happened. Hank brought home a machine that could do everything but plan menus and pay for the groceries, an automatic food processor. According to the pamphlet for our *piece de resistance*, once you live with this "mind-boggling miracle of modern ingenuity," you'll wonder how you ever got along without it. "Mind-boggling" is right. A gadget within a gadget within a gadget. It came with nine attachments. One blade chopped and sliced vegetables, one grated cheese and chocolate, one ground raw and cooked meats, one pureed soups, and one made a mousse in a minute.

The idea of minute mousse turned Hank on, so he set about preparing it for dinner that night. The recipe called for four egg whites, and that food processor had no attachment for separating whites from yolks. It took twelve eggs to produce four clear whites. Needless to say, while Hank was busy breaking eggs, the chocolate that he was melting on the stove scorched. Since there was none left, we settled for burnt-chocolate mousse.

Each ingredient had to be mixed in the machine for precisely twelve-and-three-quarter seconds. I stared at my watch while Hank ran the processor, using all nine attachments. Victorious at last, he proudly spooned out burnt-chocolate mousse for four. Unfortunately, we had to feed six. Counting cleanup time, his minute mousse took him one hour and eight leftover egg yolks.

This experience made something inside me snap. After Hank left for work the next morning, I carried all our gadgets—from pop-up toaster to miracle food processor—out the back door. I placed them in a perfectly straight line on the garage floor, exactly under the door frame.

I took one last look at the gleaming array of stainless steel, cast iron, glass, and Teflon, then stepped back.

As I pushed the button, the automatic garage door began to close, noisily, resolutely, irretrievably. . .

CHRISTMAS CARDS

The boys and I are arguing in front of the rambling, rosy bougainvillea. Husband Hank focuses, sets the timer, then rushes to his place among us. "Shut up," he says. We all look straight ahead. Without moving his lips, Hank mutters, "Six, five, four, three, two....Smile, dammit, now." We are making a new family picture for our Christmas card.

Getting a photograph in which all six of us look holiday cheerful is as difficult as paying Christmas bills in February–especially for our photographer. Once on this our third family photo shoot, he trips over an exposed root in front of the camera while running to get in the picture. Twice he slips in a muddy place left by rain the night before. The second time, he skids right past us and into the fence. The resulting photo is of the backs of our heads, turned to watch his forced landing.

We went on our first shoot when the boys were eleven, ten, six, and two. The oldest two wore English tweed jackets–which they hated. After they once had asked my mother where her family was from, she went straight to a British import shop and bought them belted tweed jackets, lest they forget. The six-year-old had his choice of inherited coats which had been worn only at Christmas and Easter and to greet their paternal grandmother when she came to visit from Holland. The youngest wore a Dutch suit, a William-of-Orange style, that my mother-in-law had sent when she heard about the English tweeds.

Hank had held our youngest in his arms for that first family portrait. He'd centered the camera, clenched his pipe, grabbed the child, and leapt into his place. After thirty-six shots, he'd bitten through his pipe stem.

Five days later he came home with developed photographs and threw them on the table. I picked one up. It was focused perfectly, and the color was beautiful. The older boys, however, had both crossed their eyes. I picked up another one. The same two had puckered their lips into a circle and opened their eyes as wide as they could— their fish imitation. In the third, they had pushed their bottom jaws out and rolled their eyes. They looked like English tweed gorillas. I shuffled through the rest of the pictures, each botched by the two comedians.

Again we took pictures, this time with film the two jokers had bought with money from their paper route. That Christmas card actually brought glad tidings from our friends, comments like, "Your boys look positively angelic, especially the two older ones."

We made our second Christmas family photo four years later in Eugene, Oregon. There was a foot of snow on the ground—perfect for a winter wonderland or an extra chorus of "White Christmas"—except we couldn't find the tripod. No one had seen it since we had moved from Texas six months earlier. We searched through nine still-unpacked barrels, all labeled "miscellaneous" and stacked in the garage. We found Halloween costumes and plastic Easter eggs. We found ornamental Valentines... and we found the tripod in the bottom of the last barrel.

The six of us plowed through packing paper, crawled into the car, and drove to a woodsy spot. The boys wore different colored stocking caps. They were now fifteen, fourteen, ten, and, six years old (the boys, not the caps).

It was a Sunday afternoon in late November. Fresh snow had fallen the night before. The trees were flocked and there were no footprints. Hank chose the perfect spot for the tripod. We positioned ourselves in front of the trees, marching in place to stay warm and exhaling cloudy air. A logging truck drove by and blew its deep horn. It even started to snow again. I had the feeling that a sleigh pulled by reindeer might come gliding by any moment.

Instead, our youngest began to cry. He had tucked his pants inside his boots, and his boots had filled with snow. The snow had melted, and he was COLD. The rest of us threatened, "If you don't straighten up and smile, we'll have to spend another Sunday afternoon taking pictures in the cold, icy snow."

He shivered and forced the corners of his mouth up. We all did. Hank jogged. The camera flashed. We smiled. Hank jogged. The camera flashed. Then Hank forgot and jogged in a straight line instead of a semicircle, making bootprints between us and the camera. We groaned and forced our numb legs to move over until his footprints were out of the camera's eye.

Finally, the last picture clicked. The snow was falling faster and the afternoon began to look like night. I could hear the squish each time my youngest son took a step toward the car. His teeth were chattering. I thought that we were not likely to make another family photo for Christmas until he had grown a beard.

Well, the youngest has no whiskers yet, but here we are seven years and three states later standing in front of the bougainvillea. The boys are twenty-two, twenty-one, seventeen, and thirteen, and the setting for this Christmas photo shoot is a quaint little fenced park just four blocks from where we live in California.

Getting everyone dressed and ready was as horrendous as ever. Each boy stole a pair of socks from his father's drawer. Each boy searched for his own shoes. Number three son wore a jacket that number two had planned to wear. The jacket actually belongs to number one, who wondered where it had gone.

At last, we were ready. We walked to the park. Hank took the pictures. I held my breath. Somehow, the family seemed too composed. Then it happened. A pretty girl none of us had ever seen before walked by. She smiled. The boys smiled back. The seventeen-year-old said, "Hi, there. Won't you join us?"

"I'd love to," she said and stepped right into the picture. The boys all looked at her admiringly. She stayed for three shots, smiling into the camera as if she had always been a part of our family.

Then she kissed each one of the boys on the cheek. Before they could ask her name, she waved goodbye, ran to her car down the street, and drove away.

The next picture that Hank took is the one we used for that year's Christmas card. We chose it because the boys look as if they have just discovered that there really is a Santa Claus. And Hank and I look as if we have just discovered that Santa Claus is a girl.

Up a Tree

Eight months ago I was saving all my shower water for the flower beds and flushing only when the toilet bowl was in a state of emergency. California was in the midst of a drought. Today I'm wearing white cotton socks so as not to grind more dirt into my rain-soaked carpet, and my flower beds are somewhere underneath the water that has pooled in our yard. California is in the midst of a deluge. When I drove my youngest to school, we passed tree after tree broken and uprooted by winds gusting well over hurricane force.

Yesterday I ran over a tree. It was standing straight and tall until I mowed it down with my white-socked right foot pressed on the accelerator. I was driving our new second-hand sports car to the shopping center to buy towels—towels for mopping, towels for wiping, towels for drying.

The sun had just come out for one of its cameo appearances, and the clouds outlined imaginary figures against the blue sky. One bunch looked like Mickey Mouse tilting his head just slightly to the right. Another looked like a salty seaman smoking a pot-bellied pipe and telling his adventures. His listener was a little dog with an Afro hairdo and only three legs. I thought I saw his tail wag.

Suddenly a tree covered my entire windshield. I'd driven into the parking lot on automatic pilot. Each space has its own tree planted up over the curb. As soon as I saw tree, I knew I needed brakes. I pressed my foot to the floorboard. The car lurched forward—over the curb, over the trunk of the tree, and over its foliage. My foot had hit the accelerator.

The car and I landed in the next parking lane, and we were even headed in the right direction according to a big white arrow. No cars were parked in that lane, so I sat up very straight, took a deep breath, and casually drove around into the next one. I could see my hit-and-run victim straight ahead as I parked. The tree lay flat, not uprooted, just run down.

I glanced around just the way I used to do when I tripped over my own feet. No one was laughing or pointing an accusing finger in my direction. Two women were walking towards their car, carrying their purchases and chatting other over the tops of their paper bags. Neither one glanced at the fallen tree. So far as I could tell, no one had witnessed the accident.

Then I saw the hood of our new car covered with little green leaves, twigs, and pieces of yellow blossoms. Uh-oh! Nonchalantly whistling a happy tune, I stepped out of the car, glancing over my shoulder before I opened the trunk to get the cloth we kept there for polishing.

Still whistling, I circled around to face the headlights and began to brush the tree off the hood. If I held my head just right, I could brush body parts off the car and see the slain tree at the same time over my shoulder. A little girl stopped skateboarding and stared at the fallen tree, shaking her head. She looked in my direction. I became very busy cleaning the headlights, bending over them so she couldn't see the telltale scraps of foliage.

That's when I saw that one of our parking lights was bent, a fact that any homicide detective would pick up immediately. Putting both hands underneath the light, I groaned and pushed as hard as I could. The light popped right back into place. I checked to see if anyone was watching. The lot was empty. I dropped to my knees and looked beneath the car. The area between the two front wheels looked like an underground flower shop.

I went to the back seat for my umbrella. Propping it on my shoulder as if it were a gun, I marched up to the right front wheel. I poked and scraped. I marched around to the left front wheel, poked, and scraped. Piles of foliage dropped to the asphalt. More incriminating evidence. I drove the car around another lane and into a new parking space, still facing the sprawling tree.

I got out and walked into the store to get towels. While I was waiting to pay, a woman came in and whispered something to the cashier. I wondered if she were saying that the woman with the towels had just run over a tree. I began to hum and ogle the ceiling, but my money was accepted without comment.

When I got back to the parking lot, a crowd of workmen were gathered round the tree. Four men were holding the tree in place while the fifth man was applying a splint. The sixth man was sitting on a cart giving orders.

I dashed to the car, holding my purchase in front of my face. When I dropped the package in the passenger seat, I thought the man in the cart was surely staring at me, but his back was to me while he shouted directions to his workmen.

I drove home very carefully and put the car in the

garage. Husband Hank met me at the door and took the towels. "How'd the new car drive?" he asked.

"Beautifully," I said. "Feels almost like flying."

OLD ENOUGH TO DIE

He shuffled toward the chair and groped for its right arm, clutching it as he sat. The radio blared on the table next to him, and he leaned closer to hear the morning news. He put one sock on, then rested.

Even though he'd lost his sight, he knew that the sock was tan. His wife always put that color in the upper right-hand corner of his top dresser drawer. He was putting on the second sock when it happened. "Sue, I'm sick," he hollered, "I'm sick."

His wife was just coming up the stairs and saw him heaving violently. She rushed to the linen closet for towels. When she got to him, he was slumped in the chair. "Mickey, don't leave me!" she screamed. Her husband's eyes were closed, but his lips moving.

She yanked out the radio's plug and put her ear against his lips. "I won't, Sue, I won't," he whispered. Then his body slipped to the floor. Sobbing his name, she put the towels beneath his head, and ran to call help.

* * * *

My father was unconscious thirty-six hours. The doctor said he'd suffered an abdominal aneurysm, but his damaged blood vessel could be replaced with plastic tubing. My mother refused. She and Dad had agreed that octogenarians had no business in surgery to prolong life, and the doctor held no hope for recovery. Dad was in the hospital three weeks, then went to a nursing home.

Mom had insisted that I delay my flight across the country until Dad's condition stabilized. When I arrived in North Carolina from California, I dreaded seeing my father in a nursing home, but he looked much better than I expected. He was clean-shaven, and the little fringe of hair that remained around his head was neatly trimmed. He smelled good.

He grabbed for my hand when he heard my voice, asking about my husband and our four sons. I said they were fine. He asked me the date and what time it was. I told him. He asked me again. Then he asked me about my husband and sons. While answering, I rubbed the top of his head and remembered how he used to do that himself when he was arguing a hot political issue. He held Mom's hand and looked like a drowsy little kitten who enjoyed being stroked. His contented expression reminded me of how he made me feel when I was little.

One summer night when I was five, I asked him to come outside and watch me ride my bicycle. He was reading the paper, but he accepted my invitation. I had pajamas on, and he waved as I pedaled in front of him, smiling the same big smile as on the day he'd announced that I had a brand-new baby brother. I smiled back.

Just then my left pajama leg caught in the bicycle chain, and I fell. My leg was bleeding, and I was crying. He ran toward me and, with his pocket knife, separated the shredded pajama leg from the bicycle chain. He carried me into the house, washed my leg, and told me everything would be all right.

I cried even louder then, because I knew that next he would reach for the big bottle of Merthiolate. While holding me tight and dousing my leg with the blazing pink liquid, he blew as hard as he could. He looked like a picture in my storybook of the old north wind in darkest winter. He made me laugh while I was still crying.

I snuggled against his chest. He told me about how little I was when I was born, about how I surprised everyone by coming two months early, and how the doctor said I'd never make it. When I made it to two days old, the doctor said, "Okay, you may as well give her a name." My mom said, "Lola Mehegan Dawson."

"My God," the doctor said, "that name'll kill her for sure!"

Then, my dad said, "Cutie, you were so little that I could have put you in my pocket." I giggled and thought what fun it would be to ride in my father's pocket while he worked at his drugstore, especially when he was making banana splits. I was sure he'd dip some bites into his pocket just for me, when no one was looking.

Now he couldn't even get well. He looked tired. My mom searched his face as if she wanted to tell him something. But she said nothing.

Dad had a private nurse, but Mom had been staying with him in the afternoons. I planned to stay this afternoon and night to give them a break. Dad couldn't feed himself. He had to be turned every hour and have his body rubbed with a special lotion.

The afternoon went well. Dad slept a lot, though he and I did have a frequent conversation about age. "Cutie, how old am I?"

"Dad, you're eighty-eight. You had your eighty-eighth birthday just before you got sick."

"Good, I thought I was older."

"Dad, how old did you think you were?"

He said, "I feel like I'm a hundred." We laughed. And then he said, "Cutie, I'm tired."

I rubbed his head, and he went back to sleep. Later he woke up and asked again how old he was. "Dad, you're eighty-eight."

A long stillness followed, and I thought he had gone back to sleep. Instead, he said, "Eighty-eight years old....That's old enough to die." I was glad that he couldn't see the tears in my eyes.

Mom was waiting for me the next morning with coffee brewing. She searched my face for news of Dad. I told her I had enjoyed my night with him and what he had said. She said that she knew Dad was tired. Tears started, but she dried her eyes, and insisted that I go to bed. When I awoke, the house was quiet. By my watch, I'd slept four hours. I looked out the bedroom window. The car was not in the driveway. I washed and dressed and decided to catch a bus to the nursing home.

Lunch trays were being removed when I got there. I met an orderly carrying Dad's tray. The food had not been touched. His door was half-open. I saw Mom leaning over him, holding his hands in hers.

Dad's eyes were closed, but Mom was pressing her cheek against his. Her lips almost touched his earlobe. She kissed his ear before she spoke. "It's all right, Mick. Don't stay. Don't stay just for me."

Public Domain

Sir Winston Churchill told us how many children to have. The prime minister said in one of his books to have "one to replace the father, one to replace the mother, one to increase the population, and one in case of accident." We had four boys in nine years.

That's the good news. The bad news is, now they're all over six feet tall and home for the summer. When they're standing, they control the room. When they're sitting, they look like they're standing. When they're lying down, they look like wall-to-wall carpet that eats.

Our house is not a home. It's public domain. It's a:

MOTEL We have excellent accommodations with low rates. Sometimes friends whom we haven't even met sleep over. The adjoining bathroom comes fully equipped with wet towels, gamy socks, melted soap, and my missing comb.

RESTAURANT This is conveniently located next to the motel. It comes equipped with a female robot that cooks, waits tables, and washes dishes. When her mechanism breaks down, she throws the dishes at people. Her aim is excellent.

WAREHOUSE This is for storing used furniture for the apartment the boys plan to get—some day. The oldest bought a sofa and one and a half chairs at a fire sale two years ago. He stored them in the attic. The dust fumes trigger the smoke alarm at least once a week.

LAUNDROMAT This is open twenty-four hours a day. Last week alone, the washing machine washed fifty-five pairs of socks. The female robot doesn't wear socks. So that means that five people wore eleven pairs of socks in seven days. The dryer ate one sock. One foot's in trouble this week.

VACATION RESORT Three of the oldest boys' cronies from out of state showed up on the same day for a week's stay. The four of them shared the motel room. Two slept from 11 p.m. to 7 a.m. and two slept from 7:30 a.m to 1:30 p.m. The ones who weren't napping in the motel room were sampling the restaurant's menu.

CATERED DISCOTHEQUE The success of this enterprise depends upon neighbors who don't object to strobe lights and loud music. Invite all the neighbors' children, so they can't call the police if things get out of hand.

AUTO REPAIR SHOP This is for anyone who needs to find out why his jalopy broke down. This shop comes equipped with tools that either disappear or rust from being left out overnight underneath the jalopy. This was originally a garage and driveway combination. It also doubles as a parking lot, and the one whose car is blocked is always the one who needs to get out.

RENT-A-CAR SERVICE This is for whoever took his jalopy apart to see why it broke down. He's figured out the problem, but someone ran over the steering mechanism while it was lying in the driveway. Company policy dictates the rental car always be returned with no gas.

INFIRMARY This is for the boy who finally put his jalopy back together but took his finger apart in the process, also for those hit by dishes female robot throws.

PET SHOP   This is located inside the youngest son's room. The World Books have been positioned into upside down "V's" so his pet rats can run through for their daily exercise. The dog sleeps under the bed and growls at the rats. The cat sleeps at the foot of the bed and snarls at the dog. The boy just sleeps.

ANSWERING SERVICE   This office answers all incoming calls for the motel, restaurant, auto repair shop, and parking lot. It takes messages but does not guarantee delivery to the correct person.

LOST-AND-FOUND OFFICE   This office maintains a good supply of empty wallets, missing combs, used toothbrushes, and single socks. Some of these items make good weapons, and the female robot throws them instead of dishes—not responsible for articles left over thirty days.

SAVINGS AND LOAN BANK   So called because any savings are repeatedly loaned, leaving a pocketbook full of IOU's which are not redeemable upon demand.

PSYCHIATRISTS' OFFICE   This office never closes and covers any problem: broken heart, bad image, lost baseball game, unemployment, broken jalopy, or unreasonable parent. If both parents are unreasonable, this office is staffed by the oldest boy—unless he is the patient, in which case, it falls to the next in line.

Because husband Hank and I are committed to each other, we're thinking of having ourselves committed—at least until the end of the summer.

Retreat with Us

Hank and I had dreaded this evening because the other couple always insulted each other, but they were different tonight. The wife of thirty years acted as if she were seeing and enjoying her husband for the very first time. He squeezed her hand while she talked, and she squeezed back.

Then it came out, "We went to a marriage retreat."

"And while we were there, we talked," the wife added. "We talked about our feelings. I've always loved Jim, but that weekend I fell in 'like' with him." Obviously Jim felt the same.

Hank and I have talked about our feelings for years, and we've never gone to sleep mad. Some nights we haven't gone to sleep at all—staying awake to debate our differences of opinion. But Hank and I were curious. Could a weekend retreat make a good marriage better?

Last Friday night, to try it out, we stood with twenty-nine other couples in a motel conference room, wondering if we would leave on Sunday with a happy glow. The leader had a beard, wore a tweed jacket with leather elbows, and smoked a pipe. He reminded me of my college English professor, but he was a Catholic priest.

Father Brown told us that this was a crash course in communication between husband and wife. He asked each husband to introduce his wife around the conference room by telling her most endearing quality. The wives were to do the same for their husbands.

Most of the men said that their wife's most endearing quality was patience. Hank said that mine was persuasiveness—the reason for his being here. Most of the wives commended their husbands for joining them in the retreat. I lauded Hank for courage, demonstrated by his having worn one black sock and one blue sock to the motel.

That exchange among couples was to be the only one during the weekend. For forty-eight hours, dialogue was to be between husband and wife in the privacy of their room, with only a break or two in the conference room. Photocopied sheets listed topics for us to discuss and questions like: "Do I see and accept you as you really are?" "Do you see me and accept me as I really am?" "When did I feel closest to you?" "What are my reasons for going on living?"

Hank and I realized that these questions were more serious than "How do you like your eggs?" We were quiet going to our room. After we kicked off our shoes, Hank stretched out on the comfortable sofa and I took the bed. We chose "When did I feel closest to you?" as our first question.

Hank spoke first, recalling an event ten years ago in Nassau Bay, Texas. Hank was in business for himself in that community dominated by people who worked for Shell Oil. He was also running for mayor—against a Shell Oil employee. His campaign consisted mostly of six weeks of nightly question-and-answer meetings for around thirty people held in private homes. After each of these neighborhood groups, Hank and I met with Rose, his campaign manager, to discuss how he had done.

35

Rose's husband worked for Shell Oil, but she'd liked Hank's platform. She volunteered to be his campaign manager because she believed in his ideas, and she did an excellent job. So did Hank. He was predicted to win.

Two days before the election, an anonymous phone call informed me that a big banner in front of Rose's house urged voters to support Hank's opponent. I figured the caller was just a heckler, but, since Hank was at work, I drove over to Rose's.

The sign was almost as large as her roof. Thinking that someone must have put it out without Rose's knowledge, I knocked on her door. When she answered, she'd been crying. Seeing me, she backed away. "I had to do it. I've been getting threatening phone calls for two days. They said my husband would lose his job. I had to do it."

"But you said you believed in Hank," I said. "You've told everyone in town he's the one for the job. That sign not only makes you a liar, it discredits my husband's honor." She squeezed past me, but I followed her out to the front lawn.

When Hank drove up, Rose and I were rolling all over the yard and I was kicking at her and pulling her hair. He separated us and drove me home, saying very little. We were too busy planning our strategy for the last two days of the campaign.

Hank lost the election. But today in the motel was the first time that he'd told me how he felt about that fight. He said that no one had ever fought for him before. He said that he had loved it and that it was the closest he'd ever felt to anyone. I went over and stretched out on the sofa beside him.

"When did you feel closest to me?" he said. "Now it's your turn."

"The night of my senior play," I said. Hank looked puzzled. I knew he didn't remember, but then I had never really told him.

It was soon after the election. I was teaching dramatics in high school. Hank hadn't really wanted me to go back to work, thinking that four sons were work enough. But that was when women were being urged in all the media to "Do your own thing." That made me think, then decide I should. I persuaded; Hank agreed.

One night when I got home, I saw something I had not seen in all my years of marriage: Hank at the kitchen sink. Then our youngest son got bronchitis, and Hank took him to the doctor while I went to play rehearsal. He even called me at school to tell me not to worry.

When I left home the night of the senior play, our house looked like a stage set after the last performance of a long run, but I felt reasonably sure we had enough clean glasses. I'd invited the cast to our house for a celebration afterwards. Hank came to see the play, in fact, he was the one who started the standing ovation. But he left in a hurry.

When I got home, the house looked like a set for "The Happy Homemaker." There were flowers in the center of the dining room table. Around the flowers were plates of cookies, dips, pretzels, and a giant gingerbread boy—with his leg broken off and writing underneath: "Break a leg."

Before I could say a word, the cast arrived. They told Hank that it was the nicest party they'd ever had.

37

They told him, and so did I; but I didn't tell him how very close I felt to him at that moment.

The phone's ring called us back to the motel room. Hank answered, and the voice on the other end reminded us that it was time to return to the conference room. We walked down the hall with our arms around each other. We had started to glow already.

TALKING SMALL

According to the President's Commission on Foreign Language and International Study, nine out of ten native-born Americans cannot speak, read, or effectively understand any language but English.

I am one of those nine, and even my English has been questioned. My southern upbringing gives my speech a twang that hangs in the air long after my words have gone unheard, ignored, or forgotten. When I asked my neighbor if she were going to the fair, she said she thought it was illegal to follow fire engines. In other words, even in America, I talk funny.

My son Ted enrolled for a night course in German at the college after he accepted an invitation to spend a month in Germany. Since he wasn't old enough to drive, I volunteered to provide transportation and, just for fun, take the course with him. That's how much I knew about the German language. Anyone who takes German just for fun has to be a person who considers a night on the town to be a Prussian military drill.

The class was small—twenty-two people. The teacher was handsome, disciplined, and very serious. I am sure that he had never giggled in church growing up. I am almost sure that he had never giggled at all. But he was not there just for fun. He was there to teach German.

Since my son and I were sharing a book, he wrote "Ted and Lola Gillebaard" inside the cover. Those four words proved to be a consolation to me all through the course. They looked familiar.

The textbook was *Deutsch heute*, meaning "German Today." The word "*heute*" is not capitalized because, even though all German nouns are capitalized, *heute* (today) is an adverb and begins with a small letter, even in a title. I hadn't even opened the book, and I was confused.

Each chapter began with what the teacher called small talk. That's what southerners call chitchat, and I've always been good at that. "How's it going? How've you been? Long time no see. Do you think it's gonna rain?"

Germans say things like that. According to the textbook, Frau Schmidt says, "*Furchtbares Wetter heute nicht?*" ("Horrible weather today, isn't it?") Then Herr Sauer says, "*Ja, es regnet schon drei Tage.*" ("Yes, it's already rained three days.") Frau Schmidt responds with, "*Es ist schon richtig Herbst.*" ("It is already regular fall weather.")

Furchtbares Wetter? richtig Herbst? That's small talk? Do you know how tight a southerner has to purse his lips to say *Furchtbares Wetter?* First I would take a deep breath and start pursing. Then I would concentrate on saying "*furcht*" without letting my top teeth bite my bottom lip. Now I was ready for "*bares*" but my tongue was in the wrong place, and I had blown out all my air on "*furcht.*" I would take another deep breath, pull my tongue in, and say "*bares.*" It took thirty seconds to say the German word for "horrible," and that was with ten seconds between the "horr" and the "ible."

Not only that. We were in beautiful, sunny California saying that the weather was horrible. I preferred to answer, "*Das Wetter ist schon.*" ("The weather is nice.") I consider myself an honest person, even when it comes to small talk about the weather. Besides, it's easier to say, "*Das Wetter ist schon.*" The teacher refused to accept that answer. The small talk was about Germany, he said, and in Germany the weather is mostly *furchtbares.*

The next chapter was worse. My son and I discovered that every noun has a gender that must never be confused with he, she, or it. German nouns come in masculine/feminine, and neuter: *der, die,* and *das.* But sex has absolutely nothing to do with it. Cheese is masculine and butter is feminine. A ballpoint pen is masculine and a piece of chalk is feminine. A young lady (*Fraulein*) is neuter. Can you imagine what it does to a young girl to be told she's a neuter? But what a nice surprise for the young boy when he discovers that she is not.

While I was practicing pursing and thinking about the boy and girl, the teacher explained that some German verbs are split. These are called separable verbs. The German verb *kaufen* means to buy. The German verb *einkaufen* means to shop. But in the present and imperative forms the verb is split with the prefix placed at the end of the sentence. For example, "*Kaufe Supermarkt ein*" literally translates as "Buy supermarket a." In German it means "Shop at the supermarket." And this is still only small talk. *Furchtbares* chitchat, *nicht?*

Next, the teacher assigned five minutes of original dialogue to be delivered without notes on Mondays in front of the class. My son and I were partners in this germanic caper. We spent every Monday afternoon crouched over the kitchen table putting German words together into some kind of not-too-boring story.

41

We were both thrilled to discover the German word "*damit.*" Even though the word means "so that," and the accent is supposed to be placed on the second syllable, my son and I derived much pleasure from blurting it out often in our Monday vocal contortions. The rest of the class laughed at our German shenanigans, but the teacher told both of us that, in his opinion, we were not too big on small talk.

The teacher was right, of course. Even though I continue to be one of the nine out of ten native-born Americans who cannot speak, read, or effectively understand any language but English, at least the German language and I have been introduced to each other.

And when my son returns from his month in Deutschland, I shall be able to point to him with pride and say, "Tell me, Son, was the weather *Fuchtbares?*"

A Proud Houstonian

She said she hoped to be hit by a truck. I said, "Mama, that is a terrible thing to wish." She went right on, as if I'd said nothing at all. She said she'd really prefer to die in her sleep, but since she lived alone, she didn't like the idea of some strange policeman or fireman breaking the lock on her door and discovering her in bed, clad only in her nightgown.

Mama was like that, extremely practical and stubbornly independent. Take her hat, for instance. I've known Mama for many years and the only places she did not wear her hat were her kitchen, her bed, and the shower. I once teased her, "Mama, I think you must have been born wearing that hat." She did not think my remark was the least bit funny and told me so. I never took her headgear lightly after that.

In her seventy-eighth year, she spent the month of November in California with her oldest son and me. She wore her hat when we walked on the beach. She wore her hat when she went to our mailbox. Even when she went out to plant the tulip bulbs, she wore her hat—a fur beret that Papa had given her the year before he died.

She was wearing a black velvet cloche the first time I ever saw her. Already engaged to their eldest son, I had flown alone to Houston, Texas, to meet her and Papa.

It's hard to say who spoke more accented English. It was my first time outside North Carolina; Mama and Papa had immigrated from Holland, just two years earlier.

We were all so anxious to like each other that we screamed our conversation as if volume would ensure understanding. Mama served tea and Dutch buttercake. She was so excited that she never took off her hat, and I wondered if wearing one in the house were an old Dutch custom. Just then, the son whom I was to marry phoned from North Carolina to ask if I had arrived. Both Mama and Papa broke into rapid Dutch with him. I didn't have to understand the language to know that they were happy with me.

Mama showed me Houston that weekend. A native Texan could not have done it better. Mama never learned to drive, but every bus driver in town knew her. She didn't even have to stand at a bus stop. A driver would put on the brakes right in the middle of the block, open the doors, and say, "How are you today, Mrs. Gillebaard?"

That weekend, before Mama paid the bus fare, she would say, "I'd like you to meet the girl my son Hank is going to marry." I would shake hands with the driver while Mama dropped in the tokens.

We toured the Sam Houston Memorial, the San Jacinto Battleground, and the largest oil well in Texas. That was before lunch. After lunch, we went through huge department stores, the likes of which I had never seen. Mama introduced me to her favorite clerks. I tried on some shoes. Mama tried on some hats. She liked a straw hat but, after perusing her check stubs, decided it was not within her budget.

Wherever we walked, it was never side by side. I trailed behind. Mama walked like a foot soldier and never tired. When we got home, I was exhausted. Mama put her hat on the closet shelf and headed for the kitchen to cook dinner. Her family had survived on sugar beets and tulip bulbs during World War II. In this land of plenty, even Mama's budget dishes made gourmet meals.

While dinner was cooking, she took out the bank book that she had started when they came to America. She showed me how she saved on her household expenses, a dollar here, a dollar there. In two years she had squirreled away a thousand dollars that Papa didn't even know about. She told me to do the same when I married her son. I was fascinated. Even my own mother and father had never shown me their bank book.

Several months later, when Papa became frustrated with his job and eager to go into business for himself, Mama brought out her secret savings. With that and a small business loan, Papa started an import company. They both worked hard and the business did well.

Papa smoked four packs of cigarettes daily. He couldn't get tobacco during the war and he couldn't seem to get enough afterwards. When he died of lung cancer, Mama gave the business to her sons. She was lost without Papa. She had always felt American women were spoiled, but after she moved back to Amsterdam, she no longer felt like a Dutch woman either.

She missed wide, open spaces and big Texas smiles. She missed her American hamburgers. She missed the friendly bus drivers. She missed Houston. When a Hollander would ask where she was from, Mama proudly answered, "I'm from Houston, Texas."

So she moved back to Houston, Texas, into a high-rise apartment right in the center of town. She decorated the walls with her Dutch tapestries and her Friesian clock. She made hot tea and baked St. Nicholas cookies. She bought a new hat. Deciding she didn't like it as well as the beret Papa had given her, she gave it to her favorite bus driver for his wife. She invested her money prudently and kept meticulous records of her earnings and her expenditures.

Mama visited us often in California. She was always glad to get here and just as glad to leave. She admitted that Southern California was beautiful, but there was no place like home and, for Mama, home was Houston, Texas.

When I met her at John Wayne Airport on the first of November, I knew that Mama had changed. Her hat was on crooked. She no longer marched, and she looked lost. Mama was so glad to see me she spoke in a mixture of Dutch and English. After all these years, I can answer in the same blend. When we hugged, her hat fell off. We laughed. I picked it up and she plopped it back on her head. When her son got home that evening, Mama tweaked his beard and grinned with pride.

During that visit, Hank and I noticed many changes. I noticed more because I was with her more. Sometimes she had no idea what day it was. Sometimes, when we were in the car, she'd ask me to drop her off at her place in Houston. Other days she was as sharp and keen as ever.

One day, she and I were invited out to lunch. When she went downstairs to bathe and dress, she was enthusiastic about the outing. I stayed in the kitchen to finish the dishes. An hour later, I went into Mama's room, and she was sitting on the bed staring out the window. She hadn't showered or changed clothes. I had to squeeze her shoulder before she even knew I was there. Confused, she'd forgotten lunch and California.

Slowly, I brought her back to reality. She told me that she had blacked out several times before, but she'd made her doctor promise not to call us. I called him right away. In confirming Mama's report, he added that she should not live alone. Hank and I begged her to consider his opinion. We talked about moving in with us, about moving next door to us, about moving into a home where she would have medical supervision.

She was adamant in her answer to everything: she felt fine and would continue to live in her apartment. The subject was closed. She got on the flight to Houston, her hat on straight and her walk determined.

Two months later, Mama was crossing the street in front of her apartment in a hurry. I know she was in a hurry because she'd left her hat on the closet shelf. She was struck, not by a truck but by an automobile.

She didn't regain consciousness. The doctor said she never knew what hit her. I'm sure he was right. Had she even suspected, Mama wouldn't have left her hat behind.

TURN ON THE TAP

Years ago, we paid a bundle for our house in Laguna Beach. Today, it's worth several bundles. But, if we wanted to sell it and if we had a buyer, we'd be forced to confess that every so often we've had to go public on our facilities.

We bought a house on a hill overlooking the ocean, knowing that what goes up must go down. What we didn't even think about was what goes down must go up and up and up until it reaches the conventional sewer system supplied by the city at the top of the hill.

We were secure with the fact that we had a septic tank, a pump, and a sewer line; to say nothing of a house in the middle of a canyon surrounded by greenbelt and a panoramic view. Looking out of the windows, we could literally watch the deer and the antelope play.

Until, that is, the morning when we heard the bulldozer groaning across the hillside. My husband Hank, hearing a clatter that sounded like a huge machine running up and down the veranda outside our bedroom, sprang from our bed to see what was the matter. I could see his mouth moving as he stood on the veranda, but the noise drowned out his voice. I joined him to watch dust from the bulldozer fly across the hill, our own wild animal farm. We stared as if watching the funeral procession of a close friend. I imagined the sad antelope and deer loping away in search of quieter playgrounds. As

Hank and I shivered on the veranda, our septic tank was the remotest thought in our minds.

The hillside was being scraped for a house to be built by an architect himself–assisted by his father, his girlfriend, and his dog. An architect builds a house very slowly, we discovered. One day I watched him hammer a two-by-four six different times before he got it exactly where he wanted it. When he finally finished, he stood back to admire his work for another eleven minutes.

That was the same day our septic tank broke down. Well, it didn't exactly break. It collapsed. Apparently, our pump was not strong enough to service a family of six who enjoy regularity atop sloping terrain. A new and stronger pump had to be ordered. Delivery and installment would take eight days.

Eight days is a long tine for six people to play it by ear, if you'll pardon the anatomical inaccuracy. As the family's only female, I suffered sex discrimination again and again. The males could lean against the veranda rail and whistle nonchalantly while showering the greenbelt below. I had to get in the car and drive two blocks to the nearest grocery store, whose facilities were distinguished only by outdated magazines.

One morning, as I returned from my reconstituted constitutional, I saw for the first time a Port-A-Can at the front of the architect's lot. It must have been there before, but hidden by stacks of lumber. Now it was propped up on cinder blocks and perched right at the curb. It was also in full view of the architect, the father, the girlfriend, the dog, and any traffic passing by. I decided to wait until the workers went to lunch.

They left promptly at noon. At two minutes past, I was standing on the curb and pretending to look in our mailbox. My neighbor from down the hill appeared, as if out of nowhere. She had a book with her and said she had been at the beach.

As soon as she was out of sight, I jumped inside the Port-A-Can. The wind caught the door and flapped it against the side of the temporary outhouse. Reaching out, I slammed it shut and latched it.

I sat, but nothing happened. I thought about when I was a little girl, traveling with my mom and going inside a gas station restroom. She had always turned on the tap water to get me to hurry up. There was no tap in the Port-A-Can.

I was sure I heard the workers returning. I pushed on the door. It was stuck. I kicked it with my shoe. It flew open. I stepped out of the Port-A-Can and into my car and drove to the grocery store.

That night, I dreamed that the grocery store was condemned because its ladies' room was stocked with outdated magazines. I had just started to protest when I woke up. It was dark and I knew I needed to go to the grocery store. I looked at my watch. It was 2:00 a.m. The grocery store was closed.

I grabbed the flashlight, my robe, and slippers and headed for the curb. I took a deep breath, stepped inside the Port-A-Can, slammed the door, and locked it. The flashlight guided me and I was relieved to discover that I didn't need a single drop of tap water to accomplish my mission.

When I was ready to step out, I pushed on the door. It was stuck. I kicked but I had on my slippers and kicking hurt my toes. The door didn't budge. I beat on it with my fist but the door was stuck at the bottom.

I heard a car drive by. I yelled but the car whizzed past. I hit the bottom of the door with my flashlight. The light went out but the door didn't open. I cursed. I wished that my mother were there.

And then I was sure I heard something outside. I listened. I did hear something... shuffling footsteps coming closer and closer. I didn't know whether to be very quiet or very loud. I decided on loud.

I beat on the door and yelled, "Help. Help." I hit the bottom of the door with my broken flashlight. Someone outside pulled open the door. There stood my neighbor from down the hill. She had a flashlight in one hand and her book in the other—and she had a very knowing grin on her face.

THE BILL

B enjamin Franklin would chuckle at the electric
company's ad in today's paper: "How To Fly a Kite
Safely." If he hadn't flown one rather unsafely through a
thunderstorm in 1792, he might not have shown that lightning is electricity and invented the lightning rod.

The same electric company also distributes to its
customers a booklet entitled "How To Take Charge of
Your Electric Bill." They do know how. They certainly
took charge of ours. It was a gradual thing. Some years
ago, our electric bill averaged $30 each reckoning pe-
riod. Over the months the $30 grew to $50 and, recently,
our electricity expenses hovered around $80 a month.
That's when I ordered the "how to" booklet.

Upon reading that one faucet drip a second can
waste up to seven hundred gallons of hot water a year, I
checked the taps, then called a family meeting to discuss
how we could conserve electric energy, to say nothing of
our money. Since we have neither pool nor jacuzzi, air
conditioner nor water bed, we skipped that section of
the booklet. We focused on our thermostat and our use
of hot water. We set our thermostat at fifty-five degrees
by night and sixty-five by day and agreed to take fewer
and shorter showers. We cut the number of our laundry
loads in half, and I consented to click on the dishwasher
only three times a week.

Our efforts really paid off. The next month our bill
read, "Pay this amount… $20." We rejoiced. For yet an-

other thirty days we practiced our parsimonious power program. With confidence I opened the next electric bill, "Pay this amount…. $256.30."

Gasping in disbelief, I sank into my chair. As I stared at the bill, I turned it over and read the fine print: "Should you question whether this bill is the correct amount for service furnished, please request an explanation from your electric company. If thereafter you still question the bill and feel you have been billed incorrectly, the amount of the bill should be deposited with the California Public Utilities Commission to avoid discontinuance of service."

I reached for the phone to dial the number printed with the instructions. "Hi. This is Janice. Can I help you?"

"I really hope so, Janice. It's about my electric bill."

"Just a second. I'll give you Linda."

Linda gave me Marge and Marge said, "Oh, you want Joan in public relations."

"This is Joan. How can I help you?" Joan's voice sounded like she had just had it scrubbed and waxed.

I told Joan my story. "There must be something wrong," she said. "We'll look into it. Hold off on making your payment." I did. We continued to jump into and out of the shower, wore sweaters in the evening, and ate dinner by candlelight.

The next bill came with a "Past Due" stamp and arrows pointing to the $256.30. The current month's bill was $95.09. I dialed quickly, going through Janice, Linda, and Marge only to find that Joan in public relations had left the company. The new person's name was Roland.

I told Roland the whole story, even the part about the sweaters and candlelight dinners. He made a couple of clucking sounds and said, "Let me look up your record." I waited. He returned.

"Your bill was incorrect the month it was $20.00. The meter reader made a mistake. This error added to the next month's bill came to a total of $256.30."

"But the bill said $20.00."

"I've explained that. The bill was wrong."

"But there's still an error of at least $150. We've been using less electricity. And we've had no visitors."

"Oh, you can spread the payments over a three-month period."

"That's not the point. There's a mistake here. We've been overcharged!"

"Mrs. Gillebaard, the meter never lies."

"Of course it does. It's a mechanical gadget, isn't it? They all lie. My electric clock runs slow. My vacuum cleaner forgets to suck. My toaster burns the toast. My washing machine cuts off. And my dryer eats single socks. What makes your meter so perfect?"

I stopped to take a breath. "As I said, Mrs. Gillebaard, we will allow you to divide that $256.30 into three payments."

"I don't care if you allow me three hundred payments, Roland. We do not owe the money."

Roland made no sound for a second. I wondered if he had left the phone. Then he said, "Of course, Mrs. Gillebaard, you can refuse to pay and we will discontinue the service." With that, he hung up.

So did I—and hit the wall with my fist. It hurt. While rubbing it, I thought about alternatives. Just the week before, I had read an article about windpower. The cheapest windmill was $18,000–provided we could get permission from the city to put it in our back yard. There's solar power, but those panels are difficult to blend into a wooded lot, and expensive, too.

Of course, I could hire an attorney at a hundred dollars an hour, and fight. But the legal cost would exceed the amount of the bill. A friend suggested hooking a generator and a bicycle together and letting my four sons take turns pumping up electricity, but I knew their increased appetites would more than double our food expenses.

Refusal to pay means our electricity is turned off. I can't even shop for better rates. Switching companies isn't allowed unless we move. So how can I fight a monopoly?

* * * *

I delivered the check in person. The office hummed with customers ordering and paying for electricity. A few moments later, the sidewalk in front of the building buzzed with people watching me as I walked up and down with my sign. It read:

"Memo to Electric Company: You are a manipulative monopoly that makes possible the fixing of prices and the virtual elimination of free competition. You also employ mediocre meter readers. From me to you: GO FLY A KITE."

Back and forth I marched, holding the sign high. The crowd grew larger and everyone was clapping and cheering. Everyone, that is, but the policeman.

THE ENTRANCE

The outside thermometer registered twelve degrees, but bright sunshine contradicted the cold. The four of us piled into the car as if we were going on a Sunday afternoon outing. Mom sat in the front seat next to my brother. My sister and I sat in the back. As my brother angled the car out of the driveway, I saw crocus blooms pushing through the pine straw.

"Look, Mom," I said. "Your flowers are blooming." Mom stared straight ahead as if she had not heard. She wore a red stocking cap the nurse's aide had given her for Christmas but her long curly hair was not underneath. Her head had been shaved for surgery. She did not look eighty-three years old, but she did look as if she'd been ill.

Mom still resembled the woman who'd sung "Oyster Stew" to me so many times when I was a little girl:

One night I ordered an oyster stew,
 all alone, pom pom, all alone.
And one small oyster appeared in view,
 all alone, pom pom, all alone....

At the end of the song we had always laughed together. She was beautiful. She wore high-heeled slippers and jeweled combs in her hair, even while she was dusting and waxing the living-room furniture. She still looked like that woman who waltzed with my father in the downstairs hallway late at night, while I tiptoed from my bed and peeked at them through the stair rails.

But now she seemed dwarfed. Her shoulders drooped, and only the red cap appeared above the back of the seat.

The driveway of the nursing home curved in a horseshoe. My brother stopped at the sheltered entrance. He rushed around to open the door for her, helping her move her legs to reach the ground. Tennis shoes and heavy white stockings were her trademark now—a badge to show that she was learning how to walk again.

My sister and I walked on either side of her through the doorway. My brother followed behind. The tennis shoes advanced by jerks. The face beneath the red cap twisted into a forced smile. She had never just walked into a room. She had always made an entrance.

The nurses at the home remembered her from when my dad was there. They smiled and called her Sue. She nodded and her tennis shoes followed them down the hall. The nurses stopped in front of her room, room 420, and we walked inside.

The tennis shoes stood still. Mom surveyed this hygenic cubicle that was to be her home. The nurses gathered behind her like real estate salesmen, smiling and chattering. My brother began to hum very softly, "One night I ordered an oyster stew, all alone, pom pom, all alone....

The sound trailed off as he walked down the hall.

Mom's tears dropped onto her tennis shoes. I put my arms around her. My sister put her arms around me. The three of us sobbed as one.

SAYING IS BELIEVING

He said, "I read your last article on the op-ed page of the *Los Angeles Times*, but for this job you have to be an expert." Desperately wanting this opportunity, I looked straight into his eyes, accenting each syllable. I said to him, "I am an expert."

"My gosh," I thought. "What am I saying? I've always maintained that there's no such thing as an expert. I've always declared I'd never employ a person who claimed to be an expert."

He hired me, right there on the spot, to direct a Humor Workshop at his university the following month. Driving home, I had to laugh. How could I be an expert? I had never directed a Humor Workshop before. But then how could I not be an expert? As far as I knew, there had never been a Humor Workshop directed before. If I were new at being an expert, at least I was free to make up my own rules.

When I got home, I looked up the definition of what I had professed to be. Wow, no wonder he had hired me. I was "a connoisseur, a specialist, a crackajack, a virtuoso, a dabster, a prima donna, a top sawyer, and a first fiddle."

And then I started to worry. Experts assume a tremendous responsibility. Since I had claimed to be a virtuoso, I needed to hustle up some very special material. Then, too, I realized that, for my whole three-hour workshop, I could not permit myself to say, "I don't know."

In my teaching days ten years earlier, "I don't know" was equivalent to being honest with the class. The students obviously respected an instructor who had the gall to stand up and answer, "I haven't the faintest idea, but let's look it up."

In all those years, the one time I did not use "I don't know" was the semester when I really didn't know—I was teaching world geography. This particular semester a strange flu virus had attacked a large number of teachers and several were forced to stay out for the whole term. The rest of us had to absorb their classes. I, the English and drama teacher, had the choice of an algebra class or world geography.

Everyone knows that a person who is expert at directing Humor Workshops is automatically and categorically no good at equations, but in my case, it was ditto for world geography. In high school the highest grade I ever made on a map test was 35 percent—and 5 percent of that was for spelling the countries correctly. Mine was the lowest grade in the class but it was still my best. The teacher even walked over to my desk and congratulated me. As I recall, her tongue was in her cheek.

Still, the day the principal offered me the choice between algebra and world geography, I chose the latter without even putting down my chalk. My thinking was that students who hadn't gotten a good foundation in geography could always pick it up through books, television, and travel. Students without a good foundation in algebra were not likely to pick it up from the morning news or a trip around the world. Besides, I had spotted a girl in world geography who was a natural.

This girl, in fact, absorbed the material so quickly that she would have been bored without something more to do. To keep her interested, I allowed her to instruct the class in map assignments while I sat in the back row and learned much more than I ever had in high school. At the end of the term I gave her an A+ and I told her she was an expert–like me.

The day I directed the Humor Workshop, the auditorium was full of people staring at me. At first I felt as if I were trying out for "Make Me Laugh," but as I talked my way through my notes, they began to respond with some spontaneous chuckles. I talked about writing and selling humor, about strong leads and snappy endings, about surprise and truth and originality. I read excerpts from humorists to illustrate my points and even read some of my own published work.

During the question-and-answer period, several people asked about markets. Then someone asked me what "op-ed" stood for, as in the op-ed page of the daily newspaper. I said that "op-ed" meant "opposite the editorial page."

I don't know where I learned the answer to that question. I've never seen the expression written out in full. In fact, the first time I heard the term, I thought it had something to do with optional editors. That was before I learned that the op-ed page is a good market for a free-lance writer.

I observed where the page was located in the newspaper. With my background in geography, it made perfect sense to me that if the editorial page were on one side and the op-ed page on the other side, then the term "op-ed" stood for "opposite the editorial page." And that's how I arrived at my expert answer to that question.

When the workshop was over and everyone had left, the man who had hired me summoned me to his office in the administration building. He said that he had enjoyed my workshop but had one criticism. "Op-ed," he said, stood for "opinion editorial" page rather than "opposite the editorial" page. Wondering if he were an expert at abbreviations, I finally concluded that opinion editorial page sounded all right, especially coming from a man whose expertise was in hiring experts. I was sorry about all those people in my workshop who would go out and debase the language by calling the "op-ed" page the "opposite the editorial" page. I blamed it all on world geography.

Feeling very much the non-expert, I left the university. When I got home, I called the *Los Angeles Times*, "A bunch of us have been having a silly argument and you can settle it, if you will. What does 'op-ed' mean?"

The voice on the other end of the line said, "It means opposite the editorial page, why?"

"No matter, but thank you," I said, replacing the receiver and looking up the number of the man at the university.

As his phone rang, I recalled something I'd read by Nicholas Butler: "An expert is one who knows more and more about less and less." That's bound to include all top sawyers, crackajacks, and first fiddles, too, I thought. I hung up the phone before it was answered.

BETTER THAN MONDAY NIGHT FOOTBALL

E very woman waiting in line laughed upon giving her money away. One woman stuck a dollar in her mouth. Another put one in the waistband of her blue jeans. A third woman tucked her dollar in the collar of her blouse. Each dollar went to the dancer who could retrieve it with his teeth. When he succeeded, the audience of 299 women squealed with delight.

These women were out for a Monday night with the girls—to see the boys. They were attending an all-male comedy strip show.

In case you were thinking "What's a nice girl like you doing in a place like this?" forget it. Every woman in the room looked like a nice girl. No one was obnoxious or tipsy, and they were all attractive. As for me, teaching has not made me rich, but it has encouraged me to do lots of things in the name of research.

Even though 299 of us were women, 300 people were actually there—my husband was with me. The two of us arrived for the second show about thirty minutes early. A waiter wearing a stiff white collar with a black bow tie and crisp, white cuffs—with bare skin in between—ushered us to the bar. He was also the club's photographer. The bar was packed with women.

Hank spotted two seats beside a gorgeous brunette, who soon told him that she thought it was wonderful for him to come. "My boyfriend refused," she said. Hank grinned as though he had just won a special award. I grinned, too, and left to have my picture made by the almost topless waiter.

When I finished with the picture, the first show had ended, and the large room was emptying from one side, filling up from the other. Hank had traded our front row tickets with the gorgeous brunette and her girlfriend. We were now sitting toward the back. Hank claimed that he hadn't wanted to intimidate the performers.

Music blared as the master of ceremonies came out in a dress suit. The tune was one I'd heard many years ago, the first time I'd ever seen a female strip show. We were living in Texas then, and a client had told Hank about the Gaiety Club. It was located downtown on a side street with a string of garish blue lights outlining the marquee.

We had parked five blocks away—in front of the city library. Who knows how many students knew my license plate number? With coat collars pulled up, we looked like two spies striding into the night. The club's entrance, more like a hole in the wall than a door, opened only after Hank had paid and someone pushed a buzzer.

I saw only one other woman in the audience, and she looked like a man. We kept our coats on and collars up as the music began. Zelda slumped out onto the stage looking like she'd never seen a vitamin. Her body was motorized so that half went one way and the other half went the other way. I thought I caught Zelda stifling a yawn—that was the most animation I saw in her face.

A man in the back had waved his drink in the air and yelled, "Take it off. Take it off." The club bouncer had clutched the man's shoulder. That had been about it, but not so here on this Monday night. The women chanted, "Bring on the men! Bring on the men!" and not a bouncer in sight.

First to perform was Noochie. He jumped from behind the curtain like Batman dressed in a rhinestone-studded, black satin suit. He was a good dancer, but after he had gyrated for a few minutes, a woman yelled, "Take it off!" So Noochie danced his clothes off—well, not all of them—he kept on his rhinestone-studded string bikini. The music got faster and the master of ceremonies said, "Bring your tips up ladies. Let Noochie know you like him." And the ladies did.

The tipping line was always at least ten women long, each looking for a daring and difficult place to tuck her dollar. Noochie was game. He danced on his feet, his knees, and his hands, while maneuvering each bill from its hiding place with his teeth. He never missed a beat The women loved it. Before he left, Noochie dove to the floor. The women stood up to watch and cheered him on. Hank said, "That's no big deal. I do push-ups every morning."

Next came Larry, the male model, dressed in a three-piece grey flannel suit. Over his shoulders he wore a matching topcoat with a white silk scarf. His blow-dried hair was perfectly styled. After Larry moved around as if posing for pictures, the master of ceremonies asked the audience if they wanted to see more. The answer was a thunderous "Yeahhh!" So Larry shed down to his grey flannel bikini. His hairdo was never once mussed as he went about collecting his tips.

64

Then came "Stan, The Unknown Stripper." He wore a paper bag over his head and a raincoat which he opened to reveal a string bikini with a big question mark in front. The women howled. Stan said, "Ladies, where are you going to tell your husbands you were tonight? The Muppet Movie?" Stan said, "How about, 'We all went to play racquetball?' That way we can be sweaty."

Stan started to dance, taking off his raincoat and throwing it to the screaming women. A woman jumped on the stage, and, before the master of ceremonies could stop her, tore the paper bag off the head of "Stan, the Unknown Stripper." She threw her arms around his neck and kissed him. He looked shocked but pleased—and still kept time to the music. The almost-topless waiter led the admiring woman back to her seat.

Every performer came back on stage for the finale. The women lined up again in front of the performer they liked best, each one full feathered with dollar bills.

Hank was a good sport and didn't drag me away until I started borrowing money from strangers. I was a good sport, too. I didn't tell the gorgeous brunette to "buzz off" until she started toward Hank with a dollar bill bouncing on the center of her chest.

Monthly Mortgage Nightmare

My dream repeats itself at least once a week. In the dream, I fall asleep on the thirteenth of the month and I wake up on the sixteenth, clutching my checkbook. Then I'm screaming, "But we've always paid on time!"

Not unrelated to the dream is the fact that our house payment is due on the fifteenth of every month. The penalty for paying one day late is $218.37.

It's been a year since we bought our first California home. Our loan is conventional. Our interest rate is not. At the end of twelve months, we have paid exactly three hundred dollars toward the principal, with only twenty-nine more years to go. Just seven of our current monthly payments amount to an entire cash payment for the house in which Hank and I lived when we were first married.

The rule of thumb then was that a house or rent payment should never exceed weekly earnings, but we were home free in 1954. Hank made $600 a month and I made $350. Our rent was $60 monthly. We paid the owner personally, and always in advance.

Then Hank was transferred to Florida. We had one-and-seven-ninths children when we moved into our new duplex, leased for $78.69 a month. We paid the owner personally, the day before the rent was due.

A year later, we leased a little house with a yard full of grapefruit trees. The rent was $590 a month, with all the grapefruit we could eat and all the juice we could squeeze. We paid the owner personally on the day the rent was due.

After three years we moved to Houston, where housing was hard to find. We thought we had a good deal when we found a house whose owner was in the drapery business. The heavily curtained window dressings were included in his price of $105 a month. After we moved in, we discovered other tenants, two-inch-long cockroaches that hid beneath, behind, and within those curtains. They gave us the run of the house during the day, but it was all theirs at night.

When our infant child cried out for his night feeding, I would roll over and grab for my slippers, always shaking them to make sure they were empty. I would stomp through the house, saying, "All right, I know you're there. I'm getting ready to turn on the light. When I count to three, I'm flipping the switch. One, two, three."

As a rule, the bugs were pretty cooperative. By the time I turned on the light, most of them were back home in the curtains. No tablets, sprays, powders, pleas, or expletives ever permanently dislodged them. We never even sent friends our new address. They might have come to see us. The owner picked up his rent check on the night it was due. We let him turn the light on himself.

As soon as possible, we bought a house, financed with Hank's G.I. loan, in a new subdivision. We paid $250 down and $122 on the first of every month, with no late penalty until after the tenth. The house had three bedrooms, a two-car garage, and no curtains. We preferred venetian blinds. We lived there and prospered for four years, until we decided to build our dream house.

To save money, we did much of the work ourselves. I laid the floor tiles in the family room. Hank built kitchen cabinets and a wrap-around fireplace. The kids built a doghouse and began looking for a dog. Two years later we finished the house and settled in to live happily ever after. We owed $33,000 to the bank and $25 to the veterinarian.

"Ever after" lasted five years. Business reversals and opportunities resulted in two more moves into two more states. The last place we sold in the East was a four-bedroom brick house with a yard was full of azalea bushes and pecan trees. Behind the trees was an enclosed swimming pool. We sold that house for $55,000 and headed for California.

Arriving in Newport Beach on September 1, 1974, we leased a house the next morning for $600 a month. It was half the size of the one we'd left across the continent. The owner had first offered to sell it to us for $85,000. Laughing at the absurdity of his offer, we declined. A year later, he offered to sell for $120,000. We refused and laughed even louder.

Our next-door neighbor bought the house but assured us that we could stay on—for an extra $75 a month. One year later, the new owner offered us the house for $172,000. By then we reacted hysterically. He sold it out from under us and asked us to leave.

The next house was in Corona del Mar. We leased it for two years at $850 a month, then our landlord decided that he wanted to live there himself, even though we had never been late with the rent. He moved in and we moved out.

Now we were afraid *not* to buy. Every Sunday we went from one "Open House" sign to the next, but found nothing we liked well enough to pay an astronomical price and found nothing to lease for longer than a year.

One Sunday, just as we were about to call it a day, we started up a winding road. At the top of the hill was a "For Sale" sign—in front of a garage. No house was visible at all, so we got out to look.

As soon as we circled the garage, we saw a house that looked as if it were perched on an Austrian alp. Hank and I caught our breath seeing the surrounding hillside, covered with wildflowers. We saw a rabbit scurry off between the blooms. We looked at each other, knowing we wanted the house, even before we went inside.

"Can we afford it?" I asked.

"No," Hank said. We were both very still.

"But can we afford not to afford it?" Hank asked.

"No," I said. We were both very still again.

"The down payment will demolish our savings," Hank said "There'll be no nest egg."

"But at least we'll have our very own nest," I said.

"You're right," Hank said, "and if we have to, we'll sell it." We hugged.

Frightened and thrilled, we signed the final papers to buy our first California home. Years later, we're still glad that we did it. But at today's prices, who can afford to buy it, if we are forced to sell?

You see, I keep having this dream. I dream about going to sleep on the thirteenth and waking up on the seventeenth....

GLAD TO BE HOME

The travel agent had tried to book me from Los Angeles to North Carolina via Chicago, but the schedule of flights from Raleigh to my parents' home in Rocky Mount refused to cooperate. I have made this trip to see my folks each year since we moved to California, and each year I've met a friend between flights at O'Hare International Airport.

We were engaged twenty-eight years ago. He went to Korea to fight, and I married someone else. So did he, and now they live in Chicago. Once a year he and I meet at the corner table inside the airport cocktail lounge to toast each other with champagne. He tells me about his new daughter-in-law and his accounting firm. I tell him about my teaching and my sons. We talk and laugh about the past, then hug goodbye.

But this year would be different. I had to meet him on my way back to California. I was to fly east from Los Angeles to Atlanta, from Atlanta to Charlotte, and from Charlotte to Rocky Mount, returning exactly two weeks later through Chicago.

The flight from Los Angeles to Atlanta was on time, so I settled in and requested a glass of wine. Just as I was taking the first sip, a man across the aisle jumped on top of the man next to him, screaming, "I'm going to slit your throat!" He was pointing a glistening knife at the victim's Adam's apple. Instantly, three airline attendants

70

appeared. One grabbed the knife, and the other two grabbed the man. He was big, and he was drunk. The attendants forced him into his seat and sat on either side of him, while the third calmed the other man and took him to a different seat. I gulped the rest of my wine.

The pilot apologized for the disturbance over the intercom and said that he had decided to continue the flight on to Atlanta, where police would meet the airplane to remove the bellicose passenger.

I ordered another glass of wine.

The plane landed just twenty minutes late, and attendants restrained the attacker while the other passengers disembarked. Police were waiting at the bottom of the steps when I began my run to another gate for my flight to Charlotte.

We touched down right on schedule, and I immediately checked in at the counter of the feeder airline that was to fly the last leg of my journey. The man behind the desk said, "The flight you're booked on doesn't exist." I asked him to repeat. He did, adding, "It's not our fault. Blame your travel agent."

Looking over my return-trip ticket, he said, "This flight from Rocky Mount to Charlotte isn't correct, either. It leaves much later, so you'd miss your connection in Chicago."

He rebooked my entire return flight, through Atlanta instead of Chicago. I protested, but he said that I was lucky to get anything at all on Memorial Day weekend. Then he said that he could put me on a flight to Raleigh in an hour. Since Raleigh is only sixty miles from my home, I took it and called my brother to meet me.

The flight was two hours late, and the Raleigh airport was jammed, but I managed to find my brother, who drove me to my parents' house. Mom and Dad were peering out the living-room window, as usual, when we pulled into the driveway.

It was a great two weeks—filled with azaleas, catching up on family news, southern-fried chicken, and lots of rest. One humid afternoon I called my friend in Chicago and told him what had happened. He was disappointed, but he understood.

The trip back to California was snail-paced. I spent a four-hour layover in Atlanta drinking coffee, wandering through the gift shop, and missing my annual meeting in Chicago. Finally I bought some note paper, found a chair, and wrote my travel agent an angry letter that concluded: "I'll never do business with your agency again." I sealed it in an envelope, thinking to mail it in Los Angeles—if we ever, ever got there.

When we did arrive, the airport was abuzz with the disaster on Flight 191. An airplane crash had killed all passengers aboard. I rummaged through my bag for my original return ticket. The flight number from Chicago read "191." I shuddered and tore up the letter I'd written. It had never felt so good to be home.

CINDERELLA'S FOOT

How sweet it was to win the first Silver Foot Award at the annual convention of the National Speakers Association. As I stood in front of all you professionals that night, you applauded, and I heard you chanting, "Lola, Lola, Lola." My name has never sounded more delicious. Cinderella was suddenly a real person.

When Hank and I got back to the room, I sat on the bed and gazed at my award: a beautifully sculpted silver foot. Then I noticed that it was a left foot, and I burst out crying. "Just what I've always needed," I smiled and sobbed to Hank, "a new left foot.

I suddenly was six-years-old and entering first grade with a brace on my left foot and leg and not a clue that that was in any way unusual. We're talking about "clout," now. You see, my mom had been Superintendent of Schools, and my dad owned the only drugstore–complete with soda fountain–in my small hometown. No one in my protective circle had dared even hint that I was at all "different."

Kids in first grade don't know much about clout. The prettiest girl in the room walked right up to me and said, "Why are you wearing that thing on your leg?" I answered as best I could, "Without it, I'd fall down." All of a sudden, I felt different.

By the time I was sixteen, jitterbugging was in but not many of the boys at the proms asked me to dance. They had all learned by then that I had no motor control on my left side and if they twirled me, I'd fall. I was well liked, though. I had discovered very early that, if I made people laugh, they hardly noticed my brace. Besides, my daddy let me bring anyone anytime for a free banana split at his soda fountain.

The brace was finally taken off, but my left foot could not have cared less. It was a "dropped" foot and, if there were the tiniest pebble on the floor, the left foot would hit it and I would drop. When my girlfriends graduated into high heels, my left foot couldn't make the grade. I bought a pair of spike heels anyway. They were beautiful. I couldn't even stand up in them, let alone walk. I wore them in my bedroom when I sat at my desk. I also had a closetful of low-heeled shoes I'd never worn. For every pair of shoes I wore, I had to buy two pairs, one in size five and one in size seven.

I had learned to live with my left foot, my limp, and lack of motor control and was rarely bothered. I walked just weirdly enough that others knew something was wrong, but they didn't know what it was. Every guy I fell in love with loved me back, but not one of them wanted to spend his life with a girl who walked funny, especially one who wore spike heels while leaning on her bedroom windowsill to watch for her knight on a white horse.

Actually, he arrived in a silver automobile and swept me right off my left foot. He really liked me, yet even he told me later that he was apprehensive when he first saw me. I'd been wearing a fashionable skirt of mid-calf length which revealed my thin lower leg and ankle above the smaller shoe. Still we began to date often, and we laughed a lot.

One time, his friends invited us to a swimming party, but Hank refused saying that we preferred to swim alone. I thought he was being romantic, so we went to the beach by ourselves. When he saw my shape in a bathing suit, he did somersaults on the sand. The thin lower leg was just that—a thin lower leg. The rest of that leg and the one beside it could have stood in a chorus line. Hank was so relieved and excited that he took a picture of me which showed only my legs.

We fell in love and married. Six months later I was pregnant. Five months after that, I was told to expect twins. Soon after I stumbled and fell, losing the twins. How I cursed my left foot.

The next year, our first son was born, followed by three more sons over a nine-year period. But the weight of carrying babies had caused the bones in my left foot to curve downward, adding a new dimension to the phrase, "My feet hurt." The pain was piercing. When the doctor recommended amputation, I was devastated.

Hank said not to worry and disappeared into his garage workshop, mumbling something about ugly artificial limbs. For two days I could hear his lathe whirring, then he marched into the house carrying three peg legs. I laughed as the tears rolled down my cheeks. One leg was covered with scotch plaid for sportswear. One sparkled with rhinestones for evening. The other was covered with Mickey Mouses for playing with the kids. That's the one I chose to take to the hospital.

It was there that this Cinderella met her fairy godmother who happened to be a man in a white coat. "I have good news," he said. "We don't have to amputate your foot. All we have to do is break all the bones in that foot and put in steel pins."

"Easy for you to say," I slurred, as the anesthesia began to take hold. Eight months later, Hank and I went out dancing and jitterbugged for the first time. At least, that's what I called it.

My left foot has served me well. Oh, I still fall a lot and I still have to buy two pairs of shoes for every pair I wear. And Hank and I have experienced the tragedies that happen to us all. But, as all of us sooner or later come to know, tragedy plus time equals comedy.

MRS. PITTMAN'S CORNBREAD

E ven though the United States produces about half the world's corn crop, North Carolina is not a leading corn-producing state. Mrs. Pittman probably doesn't know this or even give a hoot.

Mrs. Pittman grows her own corn on her own farm in the eastern part of the Tar Heel state. She grinds the corn into meal, and every morning she bakes three pans of cornbread in her wood-burning cookstove. She freezes one batch to take to friends when she's out in her pickup truck. The other two are for her cousins who help her on the farm. Any leftovers go to her dogs and pigs.

Mrs. Pittman's cornbread should be packaged and sold in restaurants, frozen-food sections, and gourmet specialty shops. But she's not interested. Her home is paid for, and she lives off the land. In other words, Mrs. Pittman has it made.

My fourteen-year-old son Ted met Mrs. Pittman for the first time right before his fifteenth birthday. He and I were visiting my mom in North Carolina. Having lived in southern California for most of his life, he'd never met a farmer.

Mom served some of Mrs. Pittman's cornbread for supper the night before we left. My son raved about the taste of that cornbread throughout the meal. I haven't seen him that excited about food since he first discovered chocolate chips in cookies.

He wanted to take some cornbread back to California, and Mom told him to telephone Mrs. Pittman, knowing she'd be delighted. What Ted didn't know was that the call would consume his whole evening. Mrs. Pittman loves to talk. His only words for forty-five minutes were "Yes, Ma'am" and "No, Ma'am." He did write down the directions she gave for getting to her farm.

The cornbread was to be ready at eleven the next morning. Mrs. Pittman fed her cousins at precisely eleven-thirty. We left Mom's at ten-thirty with Ted reading the directions while I drove. "Follow Forest Avenue round the bend. What does that mean?" Just then, we came to a sharp curve in the road—and followed it around.

He laughed and continued, "Then go to the highway." My city boy was surprised when that turned out to be a paved road with two-way traffic, and not a freeway. "Pass Bethlehem church on your left, a cemetery on your right. Then you must turn right or left. Turn left and go half a mile. Turn right and go about five miles until you see a spread-out brick house on the right. Take the next left turn and it's the third house on the left."

Ted and I did fine until the "spread-out" brick house. Used to the narrow lots in southern California, we thought all the houses looked spread out. We had driven more than five miles when houses of any kind disappeared. Only corn was growing in fields on both sides of the road.

Then I spotted a country store at an approaching crossroads, so I pulled over and went inside. The man standing behind the cash register stared as if I had dropped in from outer space. He said nothing. I thought of movie scenes about strangers lost in the rural South and remembered telling my friends in California, "It's really not like that at all."

I smiled at the man and jabbered, "The silliest thing has happened. I think I'm lost." He continued to stare at me. "I'm looking for Mrs. Pittman's house. She's making some cornbread for us to carry back to California–actually, I'm looking for a spread-out brick house. Then I'll know how to get to Mrs. Pittman's."

My voice drifted off. "If only I knew her first name," I thought. We had always called her Mrs. Pittman, but I was sure I had heard her deceased husband's first name. Male names flashed through my mind. The man rang up "No Sale" on the cash register and turned away. I could have sworn he didn't even know I was there.

"Wait," I said, "I remember–Mrs. Jacob Pittman–that's who I'm looking for, Mrs. Jacob Pittman."

The man pointed out the window. "See the way that truck's going. Follow it." The truck looked as if it were going sixty miles an hour. The man continued, "Follow it until you see a blacktop on the right. Turn. She lives in the third house on the left."

I cleared my throat, "Thank you, but, uh, what is a blacktop?"

He looked disgusted, "Lady, what color is that road out yonder?"

"Well, it's kind of, uh, grayish."

"Lady, out here we call that black."

I ran out to follow the truck, but it was nowhere in sight. After passing several dirt roads, Ted and I came to a paved road even grayer than the one we were on. Presuming it to be a blacktop, I turned and drove into the third driveway. There was no name on the mailbox, but the drive circled round the bend to the back door. Three dogs encircled the car, barking like public defenders.

Mrs. Pittman burst out the back door, talking and telling the dogs to hush. She hugged my son and me together as if we were one person, then led us into the kitchen where her cousins were eating.

Every inch of the large kitchen table was covered with heaping bowls of food: sweet potatoes, collards, butter beans, ham, corn, sliced tomatoes, and two big pans of cornbread. The chewing cousins nodded to us.

Ted asked, "How many for lunch?" Mrs. Pittman looked puzzled and said, "Just my two cousins. Ya'll come on and eat, too." I refused and Ted hardly heard her, he was so busy staring at the food. Mrs. Pittman slipped two pieces of cornbread into his hand, and we followed her into a sitting room with a pot-bellied stove right in the center.

We sat while Mrs. Pittman talked. She said she couldn't imagine my having a son as big as Ted. She walked to the kitchen door and called to her cousins, "Y'all doing all right?" They made contented noises. She sat down again—and talked. She talked about her husband Jacob, about her dogs. She talked.

We heard the chairs scrape across the floor when her cousins left the kitchen table. I got up and said we had to go. On the way out, Ted's eyes canvassed the kitchen table. "They ate it all. And they're so skinny."

Mrs. Pittman laughed and said, "That's right boy, but they work hard." She was filling four plastic bags with her cornbread. She gave us tomatoes, corn, and sweet potatoes to take to Mom, hugged us goodbye, and walked beside our car all the way to the blacktop, still talking.

Ted stowed the cornbread in his knapsack just before we left for the airport, eating two pieces while he was packing. When dinner was served on the airplane, he asked the flight attendant to heat a couple of pieces of the cornbread for him and rewarded her with a bite. He gave her another bite. Then he gave her a whole piece.

She told the other flight attendants about the delicious cornbread. One by one, they came to "talk to Ted." One by one, he gave them a piece of cornbread. They were all pretty, and Ted was enjoying himself very much.

When Ted got off the plane in California, the flight attendants kissed and hugged him good-bye. As he walked down the ramp, he was whistling. His face was beaming. His heart was light. So was his knapsack. It contained only Mrs. Pittman's cornbread's crumbs.

RESPONSE/RESPONSIBILITY

At seventeen, our third son was six feet five inches tall, a junior in high school, and a member of the varsity football squad. He had an infectious charm, a tender heart, a beautiful smile—and an irresponsible attitude.

His "harum-scarum mindset" is what his father and I called it, and we had cautioned against it many times. Paul disagreed, saying that he was just "playing it loose" and that we took life much too seriously.

When his first-grade teacher said that his written work was sloppy and hard to read, he said that he could read it easily and thought that she was the one with a problem. His fifth-grade teacher said Paul always had to bounce a ball a few more times after being told to put it away. His own words were, "The ball just bounces by itself."

Now his football coach tells him that, although he puts out top effort during games, he doesn't get up for practices. "For two weeks, you've been last to line up for stretching. You just don't show a responsible attitude."

But my son's love for the game of football took him to the Los Angeles Coliseum one scary Sunday night. The new stepfather of his best friend had given the two of them four tickets to the Rams game. They decided to invite a casual acquaintance who just happened to own a pair of powerful binoculars, but before they could capitalize on the last ticket, the best friend was told by his mom that his eight-year-old brother would occupy the fourth seat. Our family car was to furnish the wheels.

Paul got off to a late start. He spent thirty minutes looking for his wallet and twenty minutes looking for his shoes. He forgot to allow time to stop for gas and oil. They got to the coliseum at 6:05 P.M. Kick-off time was six o'clock. The parking lot was full and every space within two blocks was taken. Paul drove in and out of nearby streets, which circled into other streets. Alarmed at missing part of the first quarter, the boys paid little attention to direction.

Finally they found a vacant spot, and the four bounded out of the car. My son locked the doors and perched the eight-year-old on his shoulders, and six legs ran double time toward the bright lights of the football field. They enjoyed the game and the Rams won. As they walked away from the coliseum, my son was doing a replay of Haden's ten-yard touchdown pass.

Suddenly, best friend and little brother turned in one direction, and Paul and binocular friend turned the opposite way. Each thought he was going toward the car. Since no one knew the name of the street where they had parked, they decided to split up to look. My son and the boy with the binoculars over his shoulder went to the right; the other two went left.

It was a cold night for Southern California, and Paul and his partner had their hands in their pockets as they looked up and down each deserted street for the car. When a voice behind them hollered, "Hey, you suckers," they quickly looked back to see three teenagers coming toward then. Saying nothing, they continued to walk toward the corner. A vacant lot there was enclosed by a fence, and five young men were leaning against it. Paul noticed that one of them was holding the broken-off end of a cue stick.

At that moment, he caught in the corner of his eye a figure leaping for his back. He stiffened and whirled around, catching the attacker in the stomach with his elbow and knocking him to the ground. The boy with the binoculars screamed, "They've got a gun!" and ran as fast as he could into the darkness. A face loomed in front of Paul and he swung with his fist. The blow landed but his momentum caused him to stumble over the curb. He landed on his back in the street. The gang formed a circle around him and began to kick every part of his body. The boy with the cue stick hit him on the head.

My son told me later that he never saw a gun and never felt pain. He only thought frantically of how to escape. He imagined that the attackers were defensive linemen and he had to break through. He staggered up and started punching wildly at a body, the air, whatever his clenched hands could reach. He saw an opening in the circle and went toward it, both fists hammering.

He was free and started to run and run until he came to a street with steady traffic. He slowed to a walk, searching for anything lurking in the darkness, walking and watching. "Say, Son, are you lost?" came a voice.

My son started to hurry away, then saw a white-haired man standing on the porch in front of him. He repeated his question his question in a kindly voice.

"Yes. Yes, I've lost my car. And I've been jumped. And I've lost my friends."

"Would you like to come in and use my phone?"

"Should I? I mean, do you think I should? Do you think it's all right?"

"It's all right, Son. Come on in and use my phone."

And so my son went inside. The man called the police.

About that moment, our phone rang at home. It was our son's best friend. The boy with the binoculars had found him and his brother, and the three of them were huddled in a phone booth on South Normandy Avenue. He told Hank that Paul had been attacked, and they didn't know where he was.

Hank, taking down the phone number and address of the phone booth, told the boys to stay there while he called the police to pick them up. "We've got to find our son," he said.

He called the police station, and three times he was put on hold. Each time, someone hung up the phone before the call was answered. The fourth time, a policeman took the address of the phone booth and said that he would start a search for our son.

Hank hung up. We waited thirty minutes, but the phone didn't ring. I called the phone booth. Paul's best friend answered and I could hear his little brother crying. I told them that the police would be there soon.

My husband called the police station again, and a different officer answered. Hank explained the details, but he said, "I'm going off duty. I don't know anything about it. Please call back." And he hung up.

Hank's face blanched. He dialed the number again and explained the situation to another officer. There was a pause, then, "Oh, that's the kid that was taken to the hospital."

"Which hospital?" Hank swallowed hard.

"I don't have that report in front of me. Please call back." The officer hung up, and Hank slammed down the receiver.

Our phone rang. It was Paul calling from the man's house. He assured us that he was all right and wasn't in the hospital. The old man took the phone and gave us his number and address. He said that Paul would wait there, that he wouldn't let him walk those streets after dark. We hung up, hugged, and said, "Thank God."

When Hank called the police this time, they somehow guessed that we wanted action. We borrowed our neighbor's van to drive to Los Angeles and pick up the boys. The six of us got home at four-thirty Monday morning. Paul had driven our car back; it had been found parked seven blocks from the coliseum. The back right window had been professionally removed and the glove compartment burglarized.

When Paul got out of the car, we hugged him again. He looked beat but not beaten and beginning to feel pain from the beating he'd received. Four huge lumps had appeared on his head, and his arms were black and blue. But he was safe. We were proud of him and told him so.

Tomorrow would be soon enough to talk about responsibility and irresponsibility. Tomorrow would be soon enough to say, "If you had noticed exactly where you parked the car, none of this would have happened."

Today was for rejoicing.

FIGHT, TEAM, FIGHT, YOU ALL

O ur first son was always spirited. At age four, he hit himself in the head with the pronged end of his father's hammer, having figured out how to drive a nail by holding the hammer with both hands. Kneeling to his work, he crouched closer to watch the nail go into the wood and brought the hammer back a mite too far. The mother came running in response to the bloody cries. "What happened? Who did it?"

The little boy jumped up and down, waving his arms in the air and yelling, "Hammer. Hammer did it."

The hammer holes healed and the boy grew up. He became a cheerleader–jumping up and down and waving his arms in the air and yelling–and a student, in that order, at the University of North Carolina. While he was still a freshman, his father was transferred and the family moved to Southern California. Hank, Jr., stayed at Carolina even though his father now had to pay the chunk of difference between in-state and out-of-state tuitions.

Now a Carolina senior cheerleader and student, still in that order, Son Hank had come to California in a new capacity, as a television performer. The boy's parents were in the audience, and as they went to their seats, his mother expressed her enthusiasm with a rousing "Hurray for Hollywood!" That was the site for televising the final competition in the National Collegiate Cheerleading Championships when five squads competed for the title. That day was the first time the mother and father had seen their cheerleader/student perform with his squad.

Movie star Cheryl Ladd gave him a kiss on stage. He helped to light George Burns' cigar. (Even God has to have a little assistance now and then.) Backstage another Carolina cheerleader did a little soft shoe with Gene Kelly, and they all listened to Lou Rawls sing a romantic medley.

When their time came, the cheerleader/student and his Carolina squad performed a spirited cheer introduced by Olympic athlete Bruce Jenner and TV sportscaster Phyllis George:

> Gimme a C
> Gimme an A
> Gimme an R
> Gimme an O
> Gimme an L
> Gimme an I
> Gimme an N
> Gimme an A
> Carolina Tar Heels
> Fight Team Fight!

The North Carolina Tar Heels got that name, according to legend, during the Civil War. Soldiers fording the "Tar River" had found their feet black with tar that had been dumped into the water. Since North Carolina soldiers were known for holding their positions under fire, it was said thereafter that they stuck to their posts because they had tar on their heels. General Robert E.

Lee added to the legend when, after a fierce battle, he said, "God bless the Tar Heel boys."

The mother cried. She loved Southern California, but she's a "Tar Heel born and a Tar Heel bred" and felt just like General Lee as she witnessed the taping of the CBS television show. She shouted, "God bless the Tar Heel boys. God bless the Tar Heel girls. God bless all young women and men in the United States who cheer their team to victory." The director insisted that she put those pom poms down and sit down—she was obstructing the judges' view.

The father did not cry watching the boy perform. He was grateful that the boy was provided with three pairs of sturdy tennis shoes each year for cheerleading. He also wondered how building human pyramids and doing triple flips would help in most careers after graduation. But he clapped.

When the show was over, the mother and the father invited all sixteen North Carolina cheerleaders to spend the weekend at their home in Corona del Mar. They figured that if the boy had gone to college closer to home, he would have brought a friend home for the weekend at least eighteen times during four years. This weekend just meant that they all came at once.

The father borrowed a van. The mother borrowed sleeping bags and decided while in the grocery store to quadruple her chili recipe. The kids leaped out of the van as gracefully as they had jumped on stage. They jogged to the beach to watch the sunset. They went swimming for the first time in the Pacific Ocean. The girls raced the boys back to the house. The girls won.

The mother was so enthralled at being surrounded by southern drawls again that she forgot the chili. The father smelled it and turned off the heat just in time. That night, the floors covered with occupied sleeping bags looked like an haphazard patchwork quilt. Some time after midnight, the boy shouted from the kitchen, "Last call, you all, the fridge is closing for the night!"

They awoke the next morning is if by chain reaction and picked their breakfast grapefruit in the back yard. Three of the girls ran to the ocean for a last quick swim. One boy took so many pictures of palm trees that his eggs got cold. The mother and father drove them to the airport in the van. They pulled into the airport with little time to spare. The kids zipped into their cheerleading jackets and hugged the mother and the father. The boy was last, and he hugged the longest and the tightest before running to join his squad.

Then all sixteen of them turned around and faced the van, as if by plan. They began together, the same as the day before:

> Gimme a C
> Gimme an A
> Gimme an L-I-F
> Gimme an O
> Gimme an R
> Gimme an N-I-A
> California, California
> Yeah-h-h!

The mother started to cry all over again.

WHEN BEING A MOM JUST ISN'T ENOUGH

The pediatrician said, "Put him in an institution and get on with your life. Your child is hopelessly retarded." With that, the doctor handed Hank and me a form to fill out that would take our two-year-old son Gus away from us forever.

We drove home in silence that February day. We put our two sons to bed, then put our arms around each other and cried. Guilt pictures raced through my head.

Flash—My propping up Gus's bottle instead of holding him, because Hank, Jr., one year older, had thrown his Tinker Toys in the toilet or had toddled out the front door headed for the freeway.

Flash—My answering the telephone with a frazzled "Gillebaard Nursery," while slapping a bandaid on Hank, Jr.'s knee and shoving a pacifier into Gus's mouth.

Flash—My putting vitamin drops into Gus's nose instead of nose drops, a mistake brought on by utter exhaustion.

"Could any of these mistakes have caused the problem?" I sobbed. Hank shushed me and held me tighter. We finally fell asleep.

The next morning, I forced myself to read the three-page form and questionnaire that the pediatrician had given us. The fourth question read, "Does your child enjoy being naked?" The question startled me. Both of our boys delighted in toddling around without any clothes on. What did that have to do with anything? I ripped the form to shreds and made my decision. I called Hank at the plant and told him Gus was staying home with us.

Gus worked hard at everything he did as a kid, even play. Seldom laughing, he seemed angry and involved in some inner conflict. In the first grade he had trouble with the alphabet, so I tried waking him up at dawn to go over ABC flash cards. One morning I found him hiding under his bed. When I finally got him to come out he started to stammer and stutter. I put the flash cards away and hugged him.

His father and I decided that night that, unless school became easier for Gus, we would request that he repeat first grade. It didn't and we did. He repeated first grade, with a different teacher. She tutored Gus in the afternoons after school. He thought she was beautiful, and she praised him every time he put the letters together correctly. Soon he stopped stuttering, but he still fell over his own feet and overreacted in anger to any response that he thought was negative.

One particularly trying afternoon, I had not been able to identify a picture Gus had drawn of his brother. As a result, Gus reverted to stuttering and I resorted to screaming. Later, when I went to his room to apologize, I found him hunched over his desk like a dwarfed old man, gripping his pencil as he pushed it on the paper. He was trying to change "P" for pal under his brother's picture to "D" for dummy.

"We're having basghetti for supper," I chattered, saying spaghetti the way he said it to be playful.

"Don't make fun of me," he blurted.

I scooped him up in my arms. "Oh, Honey, I'm not making fun of you."

"And I'm not a dummy," he bristled.

"Of course, you're not. Who said that?"

"Hank—this afternoon, when we were sounding out the letters on the cereal box."

The four of us talked about calling people "dummy" while we ate spaghetti that night. Hank, Jr., said, "I was only teasing. Gus kept saying 'naisin' instead of 'raisin.'"

In those days there was no testing in public school for students who had special problems. We took Gus to a private school/hospital, which did test, and he was diagnosed as having dyslexia, a neurological deficit in the brain similar to a telephone switchboard with some loose wires that somehow short-circuit incoming and outgoing messages. Before that diagnosis, our son had been called stubborn, lazy, and forgetful—not only by his teachers but by his mom and his dad.

The Angie-Nall school/hospital cost $1,000 a month in 1967. "Forget it," his father said, "We'll just keep struggling by ourselves."

"I'll go investigate," I said, "to see how they spend the money. I could always go back to teaching."

I discovered that most of the fee went to teachers and therapists. Each child had his own teacher in a small room in the main building equipped with a desk, lamp, and a bulletin board for exhibiting daily achievements.

I recognized in the children something I'd seen in Gus many times: inner conflict and unresolved anger. But they were learning, each at his or her own pace, as they blended words over and over. I knew we had to invest in this school for our son. He entered the boarding school on the third Sunday of January. A pamphlet in his room read: "*Re: Helping your child to get settled... Make it short, happy, and very quiet.*

We were quiet, all right. I whispered to Gus, "You're going to be glad that you came here," and his father announced softly, "I'm proud of you, son." Gus just kept squinting at the ugly lamp on the table. I wanted to scoop him up in my arms and race to the car to hurry back home, but I truly believed that this school could help.

That "help" was almost impossible to measure. The school enforced strict rules, the harshest being that parents could see their child only three hours a month, because, they reasoned, too much interaction caused setbacks in the children. The three hours were a monthly drama for his father, for me, and for Gus. All of us worked very hard to make it a happy time.

Gus told me later that, on one visit, I had straightened and folded the blanket at the foot of his bed, and he wouldn't unfold it for a week, just because I had touched it. As for me, I was still having a nightmare in which Gus reached out for me in the night, but when I tried to grab his hand, he was gone. Gus was in the school three years.

Even today, twenty-five years later, he wishes we had told him that dyslexia cannot be cured; it can only be dealt with. And Gus deals with it beautifully. He is the only one of our sons who has earned a master's degree, qualifying him to work with learning-disabled kids. They adore him. His next goal is his doctorate.

Even pediatricians make mistakes.

GIFTS OF LOVE AND TUNA

The December that saw three of my sons in diapers and the dog, Dino, in heat proved disastrous. The Christmas tree fell over eleven times, coaxed by fifteen little fingers sticky with peanut butter and jelly.

The hyperactive dog tore open the reachable packages looking for the tuna fish she smelled, which was really emanating from a sandwich stashed underneath the sofa by the oldest boy while I was washing the younger one's peanut-butter-and-jelly fingers. By Christmas day, the decorations were totally tacky.

Gradually our holiday seasons improved with age, just as the boys did. Dino stopped worrying about love affairs and tuna fish sandwiches. Sons increased in number to four and scrubbed their own sticky fingers. As their father and I progressed economically, so did the quality of presents. We gave them bicycles, radios, tape decks. They bought presents for us and for one another with Christmas money they earned by washing windows, shining shoes, and cleaning cars.

When all those sons went to college, the ever-rising cost of an education burdened our budget, even though their father and I had prospered. We paid three-quarters of their expenses, but all of our sons had jobs and paid the other quarter. Two of them bagged groceries, one bused tables, and one drove a kiddie train around and around, singing, "Here comes Santa Claus, here comes Santa Claus, right down Santa Claus lane."

Not one of the four wears matching socks, and all of them eat junk food, except when a girlfriend consents to cook. To hear the boys tell it, they're paying everything and working their way through school. Their father has a job and so do I. To hear us tell it, we're paying for everything and working our way through life.

Today, our Christmas tree stands decorated and untouched in its usual corner. The ornaments are elegant and expensive and safe from kids and dogs. I'm wrapping presents, while the fire logs burn and Christmas carols play. The economy roll of poinsettia paper waits for me to cut it. The plastic bag of recycled bows is near. The tape dispenser is full, and old Christmas cards are spread out to recycle as name tags—an angel, a snowman, some reindeer.

Gifts for the boys are stacked behind me, all shapes and sizes. Some shake, some rattle, and some roll. The boys will do all three of those things to the packages between now and Christmas morn, just as they do every year. They sit around the tree and start to guess.

"Yours is bigger."

"Yours is heavier."

"But yours makes more noise."

Then they laugh when they start repeating themselves. It's become an old family tradition.

But this year's presents are the most untraditional that their father and I have ever given. There are no car keys to insert, no stereos to assemble, no video games to view. The boys can shake them, they can rattle them, they can roll them. Even more important, they can eat them.

As I look at the gifts we've planned for the boys, I remember that sticky, tuna-scented Christmas eighteen years ago and think of that bromide: "The more things change, the more they stay the same."

For each boy, there is a CARE package: twenty-four cans of tuna fish, twelve jars of peanut butter, six jars of jelly, and a jumbo bottle of multivitamins.

If Dino were here, I'd throw in a tuna melt for her.

BETWEEN THE COVERS

It wasn't the bridal suite at the Mayflower, but the bed was comfortable—and the price included twenty-four-hour room service. Every boarder on the hall either already had been or soon would be wheeled into surgery for the identical operation.

"Why does it start with the same prefix as hysterical?" she asked, "and since only women have it, why is it called 'hysterectomy' instead of 'hersterectomy'? It's a man's world," she complained to her husband.

"No, it's not," but he always said that when she said that. Besides, he was only thinking about his ingrown toenail.

For twenty-one weeks she had located bathrooms as quickly as a hungry teenager locates the refrigerator. For twenty-one weeks she had bled, sometimes a little, more often a lot, but always some. Her doctor had sympathized making clucking sounds and giving her hormone shots. He'd said it was part of the female cycle, part of the menopause.

"Then why not call it womenopause?" she screamed. He smiled and patted her on the shoulder.

She began to understand how an alcoholic's mind works. She was a tamponolic who headed straight for the feminine hygiene section of the grocery store. She stashed boxes of tampons in every cupboard of her house. Each bathroom had a supply of mini, maxi, regular, and super. She even put a box behind the big yucca plant on the patio and kept a grocery bag full of assorted sizes in her car trunk.

Every week when her sons unloaded the groceries, one of them would carry in that sack, too. She finally wrote on it with a marking pen: "Hysterical Female. Do Not Remove." And no one did after that—except she, who was always replenishing her handbag from the bag's contents when she was out on the road.

The doctor advised a D and C, and she had one the very next day. For two wonderful weeks she never once rummaged in the sack in the trunk of her car. Then it started all over again. "What did women do in the old days?" she asked her doctor.

"Some women just went to bed."

"For how long?"

"Sometimes until they died." She decided against that and elected to have a hysterectomy instead. Their hospitalization insurance had a deductible of a hundred dollars, but because of her history, the company had placed a waiver on it for this particular operation.

On the way to the hospital she said, "It's a shame that I'm spending our savings and don't even need to take suntan oil." Her husband just put his arm around her shoulders and squeezed, then winced as he had to use the brake. His ingrown toenail was worse. She unpacked her own suitcase at the hospital and quickly transferred to the bathroom the sack from the trunk of the car.

The day after the operation, the nurse came to get her out of bed. Doctor's orders were to try to walk up and down the hall. She held her stomach and left the bed gingerly. She didn't want to leave the room without her sack of supplies from the bathroom. The nurse insisted that she would never need them again, but she refused to go without them. As they were creeping down the hall, the husband hopped off the elevator. He was hopping because his ingrown toenail had grown much worse. The three of them slowly worked their way back to the room—she holding her stomach, he hopping and holding up his sore foot, the nurse holding the sack.

That's when she said to her husband, "Take your toe to the emergency room. At least our insurance will cover that." And so he did. While he was hopping there, she crawled back into bed.

Three hours later, he had not returned. She had never heard of anyone's dying from an ingrown toenail, but she asked the nurse to call the emergency room. It seemed that he had had six injections of novocaine in his toe. Each time the doctor injected him, a more serious case was admitted. By the time the doctor got back to the toe, the novocaine had worn off.

She sat in the chair to wait. An hour later, her husband hopped through the doorway and collapsed onto her bed. His whole foot was bandaged, and he held his leg so tenderly and groaned so loudly that the nurse brought him some juice. Then another nurse rushed in to fluff up his pillows. Watching all the fuss from her chair, she stated, "It's a man's world."

"No it's not," he muttered, handing her the bill from the emergency room: Toenail surgery $ 96.80
                        Insurance policy deductible $100.00
                        Amount due $96.80

He stopped groaning and she looked up from the bill. Their eyes met.

"It's not a man's world," she said to him.

"It's not a woman's world," he said to her.

Then, as so often happens between husband and wife, they said the same thing at the same instant, "It's money's world."

She wondered what her stash of supplies would bring on the open market.

START PACKING WHAT?

Wednesday is husband Hank's day off. That's when he climbs inside his airplane and practices aerobatics. Long ago he gave up asking me to come along. I have a hard enough time walking right side up, let alone flying upside down.

He left home in Laguna Beach shortly after noon to drive to the airfield. When he hit the outskirts of town, he saw a brush fire out of control on the north end of Highway 133 moving rapidly toward Laguna.

Turning around, he came back home and found me working on programs for my upcoming show on a cruise ship. He destroyed my concentration, then announced, "We're gonna have a problem."

I felt annoyed at being interrupted, until he flipped on the TV and I saw the blaze on the screen. Suddenly the cruise show was no longer the priority I had thought it was. Every channel was filling the screen with the raging fire racing toward Laguna.

The north side of our house is bounded by what is either a little mountain or a large hill. We've never decided which, but it's about a thousand feet high. When our sons were younger and unbearably hyperactive, I'd shout, "Go climb the mountain," and they did.

That Wednesday, Hank took the portable phone, a walking stick, and the binoculars and climbed the mountain. By now the clear sky was no longer clear, and the air was starting to smell like a neighborhood barbecue.

Two of our sons heard about the fire on their car radio and raced over to help. One stayed with me and the other went up the mountain to be with his dad.

When the phone rang, Hank reported that the flames were in sight but still some distance from us. I told him about the TV announcment that all three roads into Laguna had been closed. I walked out on the deck, trying to see where Hank was and feeling strange. The sky had become a blackish grey, and it was snowing. White flakes fell as on a beautiful cold day in winter—except these flakes were ashes. It was scary.

I went to the street and saw some of our neighbors packing their cars. I dialed Hank on the phone, but it didn't ring. Just as my youngest son was starting up the hill to find him, our phone rang. He said, "Hank, Jr., is on his way down the mountain to help. Start packing."

Isn't that just like a man to say, "Start packing." Start packing what?

I stood in the middle of our living room filled with treasures we have loved for more than forty years—oil paintings in Hank's family for generations—prized art objects from all over the world—the hand-carved dining room furniture. Hank built the table and chairs from solid walnut when we were first married. They cost twice as much as the set we couldn't afford to buy from the store, but what beauties.

Start packing what?

I studied the photos lining the downstairs hallway: the Christmas photo of us in Oregon standing knee-deep in snow—Hank's parents' wedding picture in Holland—diplomas from dozens of schools—my father's picture as he walked me down the aisle (He had just whispered, "Cutie, if you change your mind, just poke me and I'll make a U-turn right out of this church.")

Start packing what?

I looked at my computer filled with every story I've ever written and every presentation I've ever given, all on the hard drive, for I hadn't yet found time to learn how to save to floppy disks.

Start packing what?

Then sons Hank and Ted marched into the room. "Let's pack, Mom," and they started by each taking his favorite painting off the wall. I remembered then that just the month before, we had converted our estate to a living trust, and each of our sons listed the items he wanted to inherit. In no time Hank and Ted had their treasures packed, then they started taking out the massive dining room table. "How are you gonna put that in the car?"

"We'll tie it down on the top and put stuff in between the legs."

Suddenly struck by seriousness, I grabbed photos off the wall, my published and unpublished manuscripts and past presentations, then a box labeled "Important Papers." I grabbed my make-up travel kit and a shaving kit for Hank and a packet of pictures from last year's high school reunion. The last silly thing I crammed into my knapsack were eight silver goblets we had used the night before.

When Hank came down the hill and walked into the living room, his face turned white as he looked at the half-emptied walls and the larger paintings that were still hanging there. "Let's go," I shouted.

As we walked towards the car, our neighbors were driving off. It was five o'clock, but the sky looked like midnight. We drove down to Pacific Coast Highway, where 25,000 people were lined up to get out of Laguna through the one open road. Traffic had stopped. The darkness had turned into an orange glow which was definitely not the sun.

Hank put his arm around me and said, "Well, honey, even if we lose everything, we'll still have that month on the cruise ship."

"No, we won't," I said, "I have nothing to wear."

I'd never seen such a stricken look on his face. "You didn't pack any clothes?" he screamed.

That's when I lost it. I screamed even louder, "The car's full of YOUR art treasures and memories. There wasn't even room for a handkerchief."

"No cruise it is," Hank said, staring at the bumper-to-bumper traffic. Then he pulled me over and kissed me. "To hell with it. Let's go back home."

And so we did. Our sons followed us. Hank took the portable phone, his walking stick, and the binoculars and went back up the hill, hollering over his shoulder, "If I come back down, be ready to leave quickly. We'll drive on the left-hand side of the road."

Like Sitting Bull, he sat at the top of the hill. An hour later, he phoned. "The winds have shifted. They're going north, away from us."

I still find myself wandering through the house, wondering what to pack. I did learn how to save all my computer work on floppy disks. But, if I had it to do all over again, I still wouldn't know what to pack. Would you?

105

THE TRUTH

The truth of the matter is that every three minutes a woman is diagnosed with breast cancer, and every twelve minutes a woman dies from breast cancer. Put another way: this year about 180,000 women in the United States will get breast cancer, and 40,000 are expected to die from it. Only lung cancer kills more women than breast cancer in this country.

Even mammograms can make a mistake. Many of us have the mistaken idea that mammography is a hundred percent accurate. For all its costs, advanced technology, and discomfort, it certainly should be. But it is not. From 5 to 30 percent of the time, mammography does not pick up cancer. My breast cancer did not show up in a mammogram. I found it myself.

How? Even though there is no history of breast cancer in my family, I have had mammograms for the past twenty years. My breasts have been fibrocystic—all right, lumpy—even longer than that, but the lump that proved to be cancerous was different from the others. For one thing, it never moved, while the others did. For another thing, the cancerous lump felt warm when I touched it.

Even when my doctor agreed that this lump was there and definitely different, it did not show up on the mammogram. Ultrasound forced its appearance. Which once again shows that nobody knows your body like you do. Give it the attention it deserves, and examine your breasts regularly. Hear me?

Even when we get bad news from our bodies, there are moments that cheer us up. As soon as I got home, I called my closest woman friend. She's not a Catholic like me, but she appreciates my belief. I sobbed into the phone that the breast cyst had turned out to be a malignant tumor. She never missed a beat, "You must have gotten hold of some bad Holy Water."

She made me smile and later even brought me a half-gallon of the legendary liquid blessed by the bishop himself. The kids were not that easy. They expect mom to be there no matter what. I worried about how to break the news to our sons, then decided on the "blurt-it-out" method our family always seemed to use. When each called separately, the opening remarks of the conversation were similar, but, oh, how the punch lines differed.

"Hi, Mom."

"Hi, Babe."

"How are you?"

"Not too good. I just got bad news. The doctor says I have cancer."

Long pause. "Does that mean you're going to die?"

The second one calls: "Hi, Mom. What's up?"

"Nothing good, I'm afraid. I've just been told I have breast cancer."

Long pause. "But, Mom, you don't even eat fat."

The third one calls: "How's life treating you, Mom?"

"Not well. I just found out I have breast cancer."

Long pause. "This isn't going to bother Dad, is it?"

The fourth checks in: "Hi, Mom, "What's new?"

"Nothing good. The doctor says I have cancer."

Long pause. "Why couldn't it have been Mrs.

Fenley?" She was a neighbor who used to chase them off her sidewalk with a broom.

All of the conversations took place on December 4. The next day I went in for a chest x-ray and bone scan to see if the cancer had spread. If it had, I was determined not to have surgery. My husband wanted to take me for the tests, but I refused, "I can only handle my own emotions right now."

I spent the whole day taking my clothes off and putting them back on. Each test occurred in a cold cubicle into which a nurse would glide on squeakless shoes, take blood, or pull another machine over my chest. Then, as quickly and quietly, they would leave me with my terror, with not even a whiff of perfume to mark their exit.

Next the men in white coats marched in, with their cold hands and their vacant smiles. They poked and they prodded, then left. There were tests that day that only a a Latin major could translate, all to determine the extent of my cancer.

Hank had already told me that if anything ever happened to me, he would sell the house, buy an airplane, and become a crop duster somewhere in the world. That was his way of saying that he wouldn't live with anyone else and wouldn't be a burden to the children.

So I sat in quiet desperation, waiting for the doctor to deliver the final crushing blow. When he came into the cubicle, his first words were, "I see no cancer in the rest of your body."

I drove home as if by magic, skidded into our driveway, and ran toward the front door. Then I heard music billowing out, Mahalia Jackson singing "Silent Night."

I threw open the door. In the living room stood the largest Christmas tree we had ever had, decorated with all ornaments the kids had ever made—even the ugly ones. Standing around the tree was my family dressed in suits and ties and looking as if they were ready to carry me down the aisle in a box.

"Merry Christmas, Mom," they shouted.

"Merry Christmas," I whispered, "and a Happy New Year, and there are going to be many more. The cancer hasn't spread!"

And then I saw the dining room table, set with the good china, the good silver—even all the chipped crystal. I can honestly say that that night together was one of the best we've ever had. The family had never felt more precious, and Domino's Pizza had never tasted so good. That's the truth.

THE PRIZE

Having had seventeen major surgeries in my lifetime, I have to say that having my breast amputated was absolutely the most demeaning. The scar looked like a zipper across the spot that used to hold not only a big part of my sexuality, but also the source of nourishment for my four sons.

I have always loved being a woman, and even though I have had a hysterectomy, I did get to birth six babies before it was cut away—and I can't see a scar from it every time I take a bath. That zipper on the left side of my chest just sat there with an ugly smirk.

I had to wait six months for the reconstruction; no, make that ever since I suited up for gym class years and years and years ago, I had thought it would be great to be reconstructed. Meanwhile, I wore a prosthesis, amazed at how comfortable and cuddly it felt inside my bra and how "normal" I felt, once I put my clothes on. No one would ever have known.

Even I forgot and breezed through my workday feeling intact. Then at night, as I was getting ready for bed, that prosthesis would fall out of my bra with a plop and I would jump. As it lay there on the floor, I could almost hear it say, "Gotcha."

In private, Hank, called me "Uniboob." It was definitely a tern of endearment and his way of telling me he loved me with or without. But, somehow, the nickname never made me smile.

It was during this time that I was hired to do a keynote for a large convention in Las Vegas, Nevada. The meeting planner had seen me do a presentation six months earlier and asked if I would "wear that same sexy dress." Now, the dress had been custom made for me in Hong Kong. It was silk with a high neck, you know, the kind that you look poured into.

When he asked me to wear it, I said, "Sure," but I really wasn't so sure. That dress was the same, but my shape wasn't. Furthermore, my prosthesis could not "stand alone," and there was absolutely no room for an upper-undergarment in this slinky dress. The prosthesis was made from silicone wrapped in soft plastic, and it was heavy. Still, I felt committed to wearing the dress.

I happen to be married to a man who is very very handy. He is always fixing things. "Don't worry, honey, I can fix it," he said. Mr. Handyman fixed it all right. He attached that prosthesis to my body with Krazy Glue. It took five minutes to glue the prosthesis and three hours to get his fingers unstuck from each other.

But I did look great. I saw the meeting planner's look of approval the minute I stepped inside the auditorium. It was nothing but smooth sailing after that. The man who introduced me pronounced my last name perfectly. The microphone had no whiny aftersound. Hank was sitting in the front row with every single one of his fingers separated.

The first thirty minutes of my presentation soared. The audience was laughing in all the right places, having a grand old time. You could feel it. Suddenly I felt something else—and it was moving. A quick glance down confirmed that my prosthesis was traveling—toward my feet! What to do? I put the mike in my left hand, and in the crook of that arm, tried to prop up the traveler. But it was on the road. As it moved toward my feet, I moved with it. I kept talking, but noone was laughing anymore. A choice had to be made:

1. I could finish my presentation lying down.

2. I could put the mike in my right hand and hold the prosthesis in place with my left.

3. I could raise my arms and let gravity suck that thing right out of my dress.

I chose option three. As the prosthesis slowly moved down my dress, the audience and I watched in stunned silence. When it hit my waist, it stopped. I gave a wiggle, and it fell on the floor with a great big splat—the plop echoed round the hall. When it finally stopped, everyone was staring at me. I knew they were wondering what I would do next. That's what I was wondering, too.

I scooped up the prosthesis and stared at it, stared at it as if I had never seen it before in my whole life. "Five months ago, I had two breasts," I said softly, "and five months from now, I'll have two again."

Hank stood up and said, "Can I help?"

That's when I remembered: it was his fault—him and his crazy Krazy Glue. I drew my arm back and threw that prosthesis at Hank just as hard as I could. And I yelled, "You get the booby prize!"

THE NIPPLE

From the moment I learned that my breast would have to be amputated, I decided that I wanted reconstruction. Not every woman does, and many have asked me if the results of reconstruction were worth going through the trauma. For me, the answer is "Yes." I hated looking at that scar every time I took a bath. I honestly felt like I was not "all there."

But preparing for reconstruction was awful. I chose the simplest form of reconstruction, the implant, but preparing my body was anything but simple for me. A container called the "expander" was placed inside my chest and filled with a little more water—every week, for twelve weeks—to stretch the skin. I hated the water treatment. My skin stretched so tight that it felt ready to pop, just like a big blister.

When my skin and body were fully shaped for implantation, my plastic surgeon measured me, ordered the implant, and confirmed a date for surgery. It was to be on a Thursday. At work the day before, I was so excited I thought of nothing but having two breasts again!

That night there was a message from my plastic surgeon. The implant had been lost in shipping and the surgery had to be postponed. I burst out crying, then tried to collect myself to ask, "Where was the implant shipped from?"

"Atlanta, Georgia," he said. I should have known. Born and raised in Rocky Mount, North Carolina, I knew the old southern saying, "Even if you're on your way to Hell, you have to go through Atlanta." The stupid implant didn't just pass through Atlanta—it was manufactured amidst the biggest traffic jam in the South. It got there three days later.

It was inserted, and I looked forward to the removal of the bandages. What disappointment! My breast looked like half a grapefruit without a nipple. I had a friend who had gone this far in reconstruction and decided not even to bother going back for a nipple. Not me. I wanted the thing whole. But I had to wait until the implant surgery healed and settled. Meanwhile I had heard that I could buy a nipple at a medical supply store, so off I went.

It was early evening, right after work, and there was only one person at the medical supply store. Of course, that person was a man. Having driven a long way, however, I walked right up to him and said, "I'm looking for a nipple."

"I beg your pardon."

"I was told that you carry nipples."

"I beg your pardon."

"I've had a mastectomy. I've just had reconstruction, and I want to top it off with a nipple."

Looking completely overwhelmed and taking a deep breath, he said, "The two ladies who handle that department have gone to a mastectomy convention."

"That's wonderful," I laughed, looking him in the eye, "but I still need a nipple."

He threw up his hands and said, "I know we have nipples somewhere, but I have no idea where. Shall we look together?"

We went through every carton in that medical supply place. I have no idea what some of the things were that we found, and quite frankly, I hope never to find out. We never saw anything that even remotely resembled a nipple, so I left the place frustrated—and nippleless.

The next day, one of the store's two ladies called, and I returned to the medical supply store to purchase two nipples—one for show and one for stow. The nipple stuck on like a pasty and looked terrific. Of course, it looked as if I were in heat—constantly—but great in a sweater. I loved it.

At this point, Hank, said, "Lola, you've had so much surgery. Why don't you quit? Do you have to go back and get your nipple?"

"It's not over till it's over." And he knew I meant it.

We live in a three-story house perched in a canyon. Animals are always crawling in between floors—playing, eating, whatever animals do. I wouldn't be the least surprised to walk into my living room and find a raccoon sitting on the sofa watching television. He'd probably glance toward me and say, "Hi. How was your day?"

So—one night I woke up screaming, "There's a critter on my back! A bug's on my back!" Hank turned on the light and hollered, "I see it. I see it." He swatted it to the floor, then jumped off the bed and began to stomp it. "I've got it! I've got it!"

When whatever-it-was was good and dead, Hank picked it up between a couple of tissues, "Wanna see it?"

"No!"

He brought it over to the bed anyway. It was my nipple—or what was left of it. I burst out laughing. And then I burst out crying. "Now you know why I want nipple surgery," I sobbed.

I did have the nipple surgery. The transplant came from my inner thigh. It's kind of cute—not exactly the same color as my other one. But I put self-tanning lotion on it, and it almost matches.

Vanity, thy name is Lola.

THE CONTRACT

When we moved the scene of our relationship from the back seat of your car to a tiny apartment in Kinston, North Carolina, we drew up a contract that predated our traditional wedding ceremony. Three weeks after we were married, we invited friends—mine, yours, and ours—to a second ceremony, at which we publicly signed the contract. It was exactly four sentences long:

I promise to love you.
I promise to like you.
I promise to laugh with you.
I promise to leave you alone.

We framed the document and hung it in our tiny bathroom.

Now, almost fifty years, nine towns, five states, and twelve bathrooms later, the paper has mildewed, but the contract still hangs on a wall that everyone sees every day, just as we daily have had to face those promises.

I promise to love you.

What an easy vow that was to keep when you and I first started our life together. We kissed and craved each other like two magnets that have no choice except to press together. We were liberated and yet enslaved—free spirits in bondage only to each other. We were very, very happy.

Our joy increased when we learned that a new life was growing inside me. You promised to help when the

117

baby arrived. You couldn't feed him, for only I had that equipment, but you burped him, bounced him, and sang to him when he insisted on staying awake after his two o'clock feeding. You wore him on your shoulder like a wobbly little mouse and even designed a loss-proof pacifier with soft plastic that comfortably encircled his head. He looked as if he'd dropped in from outer space, but he sucked contentedly, then he slept—and so did we. Only we didn't make love so feverishly then. We were too tired.

I promise to like you.

I hated you that Saturday afternoon in Houston when you drove up the driveway in a new car. We had two sons by then and no money. I had quit teaching six months earlier, and we'd started a new business together, importing lumber from Scandinavia. It was thriving, but our cash flow was zero. Just that week, we'd paid the bills and our employees, but we couldn't pay ourselves. We had no cash for groceries.

But that's not why I hated you. I hated you because you were driving a Cadillac sedan which you'd just bought. True, our old car was heating up and using oil— but a Lido-lavender Cadillac? Lido-lavender is a hue that cannot be found now on even the most comprehensive color chart. I've never seen another car, or anything else, painted quite that same garish shade of purple. The car, I discovered later, actually glowed in the dark—no doubt why it was, "No money down, four years to pay."

Now we had a Cadillac in the driveway, but only bread, raisins, and peanut butter in the cupboard. I kicked the front wheel. Then I kicked you and cried. You put your arms around me. You packed a lunch of peanut-butter sandwiches and raisins, and the four of us went for a picnic in our new car. I began to like you again.

I promise to laugh with you.

The Cadillac served us well and the lumber business that we partnered soon made enough money for us to have jelly with our peanut butter. Along the way, we parented two more sons, for whom you fashioned more unique, wraparound pacifiers. Weekdays, when the boys were young, I did much of my work for the business at home. It was closed on Saturdays, so you stayed home to enjoy the children while I celebrated "my" day off.

I took belly-dancing lessons. I took guitar lessons. I browsed through the city library. I rummaged in antique shops. I took a course in meditation and joined a women's issues group.

One Saturday, I packed a suitcase while you were helping the boys put together a puzzle from the cereal box. I even managed to tuck two champagne flutes among the clothing before telling you all good-bye. At the first public telephone booth, I stopped and called our baby-sitter. Then I bought a bottle of champagne and a crock of cheese and drove to the quaint little inn where I had booked a room. After unpacking and icing the champagne, I telephoned your best friend. He called you. I waited an hour, then went downstairs to the bar.

You were sitting at the bar facing the door, so as to see your friend arrive. When I walked in and took the stool beside you, you looked astonished, then grinned. "Did anyone ever tell you that you have a beautiful smile?" I asked. We both burst out laughing. "Yes," you said softly, "someone once told me that a long time ago."

Later, you said that the weekend was the nicest surprise you'd ever had.

I promise to leave you alone.

It's nice when you're away on a business trip. I don't have to wonder what to fix for dinner or be available just because you have a new idea to discuss. Not that I don't love you and miss you and want you. Yet, it's kind of fun to have the bed and the newspaper all to myself.

The night before last, I feel asleep on the sofa with a paint brush in my hand. I had finally finished that still-life I'd started so many months ago. Yesterday, I phoned an old friend and talked for two hours.

When you came home late tonight, I made a pot of coffee, and we held hands across the table. You told me about your week and I told you about mine. By then, it was well past bedtime. I was reaching for the toothpaste in the bathroom when my eyes came to rest on our contract, now yellowed by time.

I reread our four promises and realized that we'd struck a pretty good bargain, after all.